Crazy Diamond

Crazy Diamond

SYD BARRETT

& the Dawn of Pink Floyd

Mike Watkinson & Pete Anderson

OMNIBUS PRESS
LONDON · NEW YORK · SYDNEY

First published © 1991 Omnibus Press
This edition Copyright © 1993 Omnibus Press
(A Division of Book Sales Limited)

Edited by Chris Charlesworth
Cover & Book designed by Robert Fairclough
Picture research by Mike Watkinson, Pete Anderson and David Brolan
Discography by Andy Mabbett

ISBN: 0-7119-3678-1
Order No: OP 46085

Exclusive Distributors
Book Sales Limited,
8/9 Frith Street,
London, W1V 5TZ, UK.

Music Sales Corporation,
257 Park Avenue South,
New York, NY 10010, USA.

Music Sales Pty Limited
120 Rothschild Avenue,
Rosebery, NSW 2018, Australia

To the Music Trade only:
Music Sales Limited,
8/9 Frith Street,
London W1V 5TZ, UK.

Every effort has been made to trace the copyright holders of the photographs in this
book but one or two were unreachable. We would be grateful if the photographers
concerned would contact us.

Printed and bound in Great Britain by
Redwood Books, Trowbridge, Wiltshire

A catalogue record for this book is available from the British Library.

Contents

S yd Barrett was the first psychic pop writer to rival John Lennon. That he fell into an abyss of his own making has never been disputed, but it is important to understand why and how this happened.

The cramping restrictions of being forced too soon into a narrow commercial mould caused unbearable pain to Barrett – it is almost impossible for an artist to limit himself to the attainable – but the attainable was just what the other members of Pink Floyd required. When he came to this knowledge, I believe Syd Barrett's tenuous grasp on reality was lost – he fell down into the void. It was Artistic Death and a tragedy of legendary proportions.

With little creative input from his cohorts in Pink Floyd, Syd Barrett was running on intuition alone. True, without Waters, Mason and Wright he may never have even made a record. But with them, unfortunately, Barrett was destined to be sacrificed to the pressure of the outside world.

To claim, however, that Barrett's short-lived career was a failed quest would be to deny those blazing instants which he has left with us today. Twenty-four years after his first recording, Syd Barrett's mythology is more intact than ever – a True Genius.

Julian Cope of Lambeth, July 1990.

Some critics have compared Syd Barrett to a modern-day Rimbaud, others dismiss him as a deranged psychedelic doodler, but the enigmatic founder of Pink Floyd remains one of rock's most enduring, and confounding, legends.

And the debate shows no sign of diminishing. April of 1993 saw the release of a box set containing Syd's two legendary solo albums, the retrospective 'Opel' collection of rarities and 19 Barrett outtakes. The set, appropriately titled 'Crazy Diamond – The Complete Syd Barrett', received mixed reviews but, more importantly, substantial and earnest reviews of a length and gravity normally devoted to artists with ongoing careers, high profiles and large followings who buy their records by the million.

For today, over 20 years after his musical career ended with a shambolic performance at the Cambridge Corn Exchange, the myths surrounding Barrett continue to flourish.

Syd 'sightings' are still reported in the music press with the same eccentric regularity as retired colonels report the first cuckoo of spring to The Times. Occasional 'snatch' photographs of Syd, now a middle-aged and rather stout chap with thinning cropped hair and a complete lack of concern for sartorial matters, are poured over with the same kind of interest that recent pictures of Lord Lambton might attract.

Shortly before the publication of the first edition of this book in 1991, the latest spate of rumours had him alternatively working in a Chelsea wine bar or in a Cambridge shop. In

1986 it was even alleged that he had been found dead in a Cambridge shop doorway. Happily, according to his family whose help in the writing of this book has been invaluable, Syd is very much alive and well and is enjoying a quiet life away from the pressures of stardom.

What is beyond any doubt whatsoever is that Barrett's inflence on the early Pink Floyd was immeasurable. He was their singer, lead guitarist and principal songwriter, composing eight of the 11 songs on their début album and co-writing two of the other three. He wrote the group's two early hit singles 'Arnold Layne' and 'See Emily Play' and their B-sides. He even dreamed up the group's name.

Barrett and his Cambridge friends were among the first in Britain to experiment with the so-called mind-expanding drug LSD. Amid mounting pressure to repeat the early chart success, Barrett turned increasingly to drugs for escape. The third single 'Apples And Oranges' failed to make the charts and by the time Floyd set off on a disastrous American tour, their leader was a shadow of his former self.

He left the group, quietly and in somewhat mysterious circumstances, in April 1968, and from that point on the legend of Syd Barrett grew and grew. It was fired by half-truths, apocrypha and pure lies which blended in an ever-increasing spiral of exaggeration until Syd's name became synonymous with drug-induced madness. Fanzines were launched to laud his work and the classic Pink Floyd track 'Shine On You Crazy Diamond', with lyrics inspired by Barrett's demise, fanned the flames still further. He became and remains the most celebrated acid casualty in British rock.

It is no exaggeration to suggest that his abrupt departure from Pink Floyd could be compared to John Lennon quitting The Beatles after 'She Loves You' and returning to Liverpool to live in seclusion with his Aunt Mimi, or Pete Townshend leaving The Who after 'My Generation' and settling down to run a greengrocers' shop on the Isle of Wight.

What intrigued us about the Syd Barrett story was how such a legend could have grown up around someone whose entire recorded output, including his later solo work, amounted to little more than three albums. The ultimate irony is that an undoubtedly talented young songwriter is today remembered principally for his semi-authenticated acts of lunacy. This book is an attempt to put the record straight.

Barrett-hunts have become at best irritating and at worst the hounding of a somewhat confused person for voyeuristic pleasure. We hope that by clearing up much of the mystery that surrounds Syd Barrett, he will be left in relative peace.

Mike Watkinson and Pete Anderson, June 1993.

Acknowledgements

Special thanks to the following: The Barrett family, particularly Paul and Rosemary Breen, Dave Gilmour, Pete Townshend, Storm Thorgeson, Gayla Pinion, the late Malcolm Jones, Duggie Fields, Bernard White, Geoff Mott, John Gordon, Ian Moore (Imo), Libby Chisman, Chris Dennis, the late Pip Carter, Clive Welham, Pat Beesley (*Torquay Herald Express*), Bob Klose, Andrew King, Pete Jenner, Robyn Hitchcock, all at *The Amazing Pudding*, Hugh Fielder, Rob Partridge, the late Chris 'Chimp' Chamberlain, Dan Treacey (TV Personalities), Captain Sensible, John Alder (Twink), Mike Read, Peter Mitchell (*Cambridge Evening News*), Jack Monck, Jenny Noshad, Dave Gilbert, Tim Francis, Mick Leonard, David Wingrove, Chris Dennis, Steven Pyle, Jerry Shirley, Mary Waters, Norman Smith, Keith West, Pete Brown, Jack Bruce, John Tobler, George Barlow, Nigel Lesmoire-Gordon, Nicky Campbell, Chris Charlesworth, Ivor Trueman, Rob Swift . . . and not forgetting Syd who brought us all together.

For more information about *The Amazing Pudding* send SAE or IRC to 67 Cramlington Road, Great Barr, Birmingham, B42 2EE, England.

This book is dedicated to our families and friends.

Love and thanks to Sue Geatches and Louise Cunliffe for typing services beyond the call of duty.

Chapter One

Remember When You Were Young

R oger Keith Barrett was born at 60 Glisson Road, Cambridge, on January 6, 1946, the fourth of five children raised by Dr Arthur Max Barrett and his wife Winifred. He was a dark-haired child with laughing eyes who resembled his father more closely than the rest of the brood, inheriting not only Dr Barrett's artistic ability and love of music but also his exceptionally warm personality.

Roger was a good-looking youngster, blessed with a lively and magnetic personality which enabled him to gather friends effortlessly. He drew well from an early age but seemed destined for a career in music from the day he won a piano duet at Cambridge Guildhall, playing 'The Blue Danube' with his younger sister.

Dr Barrett was a member of the Cambridge Philharmonic Society and there was always music in the household. He was a popular figure in the town where he worked as a university and hospital pathologist following a brilliant university career in London. Addenbrooke's Hospital in Cambridge contains a Barrett Room to this day.

An artistic man who painted watercolours, he wrote several books on fungi; a subject on which he was regarded as one of the country's leading authorities, and in which he drew his own illustrations.

It was while working in the wards and labs of the London Hospital that he married catering manageress Winifred Flack, great granddaughter of London's first woman mayor, Elizabeth Garrett Anderson. At 31, Winifred was five years his senior.

The circumstances of their meeting were a long-standing family joke. Both keen Scouters, they met on top of a haystack during an outing in the Essex countryside on a scorching summer day in 1930. They were married in Balham, South London, five years later.

In 1938 Dr Barrett was appointed University Demonstrator in Pathology at Cambridge. As a former pupil of the town's High School, he felt he was returning home and back in Cambridge he and his wife proceeded to raise a large family. Alan, the first child, was born in 1937 and Donald, Ruth, Roger and Rosemary would follow before the family moved into a larger house at 183 Hills Road in 1950.

By then Roger was four-years-old and already developing a highly individual streak – his sunny and good-natured temperament could occasionally be replaced by extravagant shows of petulance on not getting his own way.

On one occasion the precocious toddler grew increasingly restless when his mother kept forgetting to buy him a toy during an excessively boring shopping trip. Master Barrett's patience finally snapped when he spotted her buying a cabbage for tea. Startled Cambridge shoppers were treated to the memorable sight of an embarrassed Mrs Barrett being castigated by her enraged offspring screaming: "That's typical! You always think of yourself!"

Such outbursts were not typical however, and Roger was invariably regarded as the clown of the family, the one who kept everyone laughing during tedious motor trips to South Wales where the Barretts had a lease on a holiday cottage at Tenby.

His closest companion during these early days was his younger sister Rosemary. He doted on her even though their personalities were completely different. "He drew from an early age, mostly people, and they were always very good," she says. "At night we used to have cups of hot milk in bed and after our light was turned out he would sit up and start conducting an imaginary orchestra. The music was in his head even then.

"He didn't have any special friend. He had lots and gathered them without trying. All our mother's friends fell for him. They'd come in and ask: 'How's my boyfriend today, then?' He was lively, funny and had a magnetic personality which made him attractive to all ages.

"Encouraged by our parents, he became a Cub and later a Scout. When he was at Scouts they used to hold 'find the feather' evenings at our house. I remember him coming in to search the room and pulling handfuls of my hair out in his attempts to find the feather.

"He was always a law unto himself. Once, on holiday in North Wales, he got lost up Snowdon. We all went for a walk and he just went off on his own. He came down about an hour later to find the rest of us panicking and on the point of calling out the mountain rescue team. You never knew what he was going to do next."

Shortly after the family moved to Hills Road, Roger was sent to Morley Memorial Junior School only a few yards away. He quickly came to the attention of a teacher called Mary Waters who, having been widowed during the war, was struggling to bring up her sons John and Roger single-handed in a house in nearby Rock Road.

"He was always a very individualistic young boy," recalls Mary Waters. "Win was a marvellous mother and the home was always a very happy one. He was always the one his mum had to bother about rather than the others.

"He ran in the school sports and could run quite fast in fact. I always found him very cheerful but he went through a stage when he had a phobia about school and they had trouble getting him to return there."

At 11 Roger Barrett graduated to Cambridge High School and showed a great deal of promise with his art. The teachers at Morley had despaired of Barrett Minor who demonstrated neither interest nor enthusiasm for his schoolwork. Art was the notable exception and after passing his 11-plus (the examination which graded British school children of that time into the higher Grammar School stream or the less prestigious Secondary Schools) he was encouraged by his mother to take art lessons at Homerton College opposite his home.

It was 1957 and Britain was in the grip of the first 20th century teenage revolution. Overnight, or so it seemed, conventional British values were being eroded and replaced by an alarming American vocabulary which included alien words like 'juke-box', 'teddy boy' and 'rock 'n' roll'.

The focal point of this tidal wave of American depravity was a 21-year-old truck driver turned singer from Memphis, Tennessee, whose suggestive movements first scandalised

God-fearing fellow countrymen and later did the same for the rest of the world. It was the fate of Elvis Aaron Presley to trigger off a revolution that spread throughout the Western world, reaching even as far as the genteel seat of academia that was Cambridge.

In the wake of rock 'n' roll came the great skiffle craze. Inspired by Britain's top skiffler Lonnie Donegan, adolescent boys throughout the country formed groups by stealing mum's washboard for percussion and fixing a broom handle to a tea chest strung with wire which became a rudimentary double bass.

Roger watched with interest as his elder brother Alan played sax in a skiffle group and, inspired by his example, took up playing the ukulele. While the mere mention of rock 'n' roll was still likely to make most middle-class British parents recoil in horror, the liberal-minded Barretts actively encouraged their youngest son's burgeoning musical interests.

Typically, like boys the length and breadth of Britain, he began fashioning a small quiff with lashings of Brylcreem. Less typically, he never showed a glimmer of interest in Presley; from the age of 12 his idols were Chuck Berry, Bo Diddley and Buddy Holly.

Cambridge High School, or The County as everyone called it, remained a comforting pillar of respectability, relatively unaffected by the social upheavals of the late fifties. In 1957 it still held strong Victorian values and anyone not wearing the school cap or uniform would be sent home in disgrace as punishment.

When he reached High School, Roger's future was already mapped out – in his own mind at least. All he wanted was to paint. The tedious Latin lessons, time and energy-consuming cross-country runs and other wearisome activities were all endured or avoided until the moment he could settle down with canvas, paint and brushes.

Teachers considered him generally pleasant and helpful if occasionally a little casual and ill-disciplined. Here was someone who was clearly not going to follow in the footsteps of his more academic brothers and who deliberately flouted authority by turning up at lessons minus tie and blazer.

He would be sternly admonished and finally sent home to locate the missing garment. The Barrett home was less than a hundred yards from the school gates but the trip would sometimes take up to an hour as the budding Picasso invariably sneaked into his playroom for some illicit painting instead of returning immediately.

His closest friend and fellow conspirator at the time was a pale slender boy called John Gordon whose father worked in the local Pye electronics factory. Having suffered a traditionally strict upbringing, he noted with some envy the relaxed and informal atmosphere of the Barrett household.

"The older children had left home so Roger virtually had the run of the entire house," he remembers. "He had this massive playroom with a gramophone and sometimes it seemed his mother was his servant. Once or twice he told her to piss off and she just laughed. She loved it.

"When we were at school, the games master would send us off on a cross-country run. Some of the boys would sneak off into the woods for a quick fag but Roger would pop into his house, do a bit of painting, then come back and tag along with the stragglers. He was quite a healthy specimen but he wasn't really interested."

By the time he was 14, Roger's interest in music had reached the same obsessive level. Leaving his half-hearted attempts at being a teddy-boy behind him, for once in his life he followed the teenage trend and begged his parents for a guitar.

An acoustic instrument was bought at once and Barrett, Gordon and cohorts spent long hours in Winifred's living room endlessly listening to the same Shadows or Buddy Holly records and attempting to play along to them.

Their only interruption was when a beaming Mrs Barrett appeared with a tray of tea and cakes. As their primitive instruments had seemingly been banned from just about every other Cambridge household, word spread like wildfire that far from being frowned upon, would-be rock 'n' rollers were positively welcomed at 183 Hills Road.

A somewhat bemused Mrs Barrett soon had the impression that whenever she popped her head into the makeshift music room, the number of music-mad teenagers had doubled. Before long the Barrett home had been transformed into an informal club. On Sunday afternoons it became the place to go.

Roger's old playroom now had the atmosphere of a coffee bar as the teenagers chatted, smoked, listened to records or proudly showed off their new guitars. Occasionally Barrett and Gordon would launch into an impromptu jam while a fellow named Clive Welham thrashed out a vague sort of rhythm with a couple of knives on a biscuit tin. They called themselves The Hollerin' Blues.

Welham was an amiable working class youth of 17 who had won a scholarship to Cambridge's private school, The Perse. Sometimes he would bring along a fellow pupil who, despite his tender years, would soon develop a reputation as a local heart-throb. The guy was only 14 but he was already a competent guitar player whose future was destined to be inexorably linked with Roger Barrett's. His name was David Gilmour.

Dave Gilmour was born on March 6, 1946 (not 1944, as usually stated); one of four children of Doug and Sylvia Gilmour, who had raised their family at Grantchester Meadows, a well-to-do housing estate on the banks of the River Cam (later immortalised by a Roger Waters' song on Pink Floyd's 'Ummagumma' album).

Bearded academic Doug Gilmour was a doctor in genetics who eventually joined the 'brain drain' to the United States. His wife was a film editor who shared his concern over the growing amount of time their second son spent hunched over his new guitar painstakingly working his way through The Shadows' 'Apache' and oblivious to the world around him.

David was a quiet, rather odd-looking character with Jaggeresque lips who stood out at The Perse. The looks which would cause flutters in many a female heart were only developing. As one childhood friend recalls: "It took a while for his face to fill out and accommodate those lips."

On the other side of town, where Barrett and companions bemoaned the petty rules at The County, Gilmour's lot was even worse. The stern-faced masters at The Perse made the atmosphere at The County seem positively laid-back. Among the various indignities Gilmour had to endure were Saturday morning lessons and interminable prep sessions. Pupils were even expected to wear their caps in the streets, although sixth-formers were permitted to wear straw boaters on special occasions.

Barrett and Gilmour hit it off at once and could soon be found using a Scout hut at nearby Pern Road for rehearsals.

By now everyone apart from his family was calling Roger 'Syd' – a nickname he had picked up at the Riverside Jazz Club which met in a local pub on Friday nights. The members, mainly trenchant jazz purists in their thirties and forties, were slightly taken aback by the appearance of this thoughtful schoolboy who seemed content to simply sit in a corner and watch them meander through their set.

One of the club's mainstays was an ancient drummer called Sid Barrett. It didn't take the jazzmen long to discover that 'Sid The Beat' had a namesake and they soon began referring to both the widely-differing Barretts as Sid, though, perhaps as a means of distinction, Roger's pseudonym was always spelt with a 'y'.

The nickname was quickly picked up by Roger's schoolmates, although he did not like it himself and rarely used it.

"From the time I came to know him until the time he 'turned', Syd was fantastic," says Gilmour. "There wasn't a single person who didn't like him, think he was brilliant, or wasn't certain he was going to be a success at something. He was good-looking and fantastically talented at anything he cared to put his hand to. He was also one of the funniest people I've ever come across. When he wanted to, he could be really witty and surreal."

Members of the opposite sex clearly thought so too. By the age of 15, Syd was heavily into girls and attracting admiring glances from females two or three years his senior. His first serious relationship was with a petite brunette a few months younger than himself whose hair, cut in an unfashionable German bob, made her stand out on the streets of Cambridge. She was called Libby Gausden.

Libby could not understand what Syd saw in her but her hopes soared when a friend revealed Syd had confided that Libby would be his ideal girl . . . "if it wasn't for her freckles."

Sometimes she felt it was only a game of cat and mouse. She was just beginning to lose heart when, that June, they bumped into one another at the Cambridge public baths.

"They ought to have people like you on Dairy Box," said Syd. He clearly felt his new-found bathing beauty was fit to grace any chocolate box advertisement.

So began a three-year romance that would have its fair share of ups and downs. Like all Syd's subsequent affairs, his relationship with Libby was tempestuous. He enjoyed the company of women, so Libby's often justified possessiveness was the cause of many rows between them. Usually Syd would stalk off and not speak to her for weeks afterwards as punishment. Despite this, their relationship, which at one point almost culminated in marriage, survived until Syd moved up to London to study art at Camberwell in 1964, when they began to see much less of each other.

Right from the start Libby was awed by his original dress sense and cruel, sardonic sense of humour. Syd was already well on the way to cult status, at least among Cambridge youngsters. Occasionally he would accompany Libby or his sister to Peak's record store wearing sunglasses in the middle of winter, leading older people to think he was blind.

He began to take great pride in his appearance, buying clothes from Oxfam and adapting them to his own tastes. His hair, long by 1961 standards, was also terribly important. "You must wash it until it squeaks," he'd tell Libby.

"He looked like an art student and never conformed," she says. "He had an oiled knitted fisherman's sweater, the type that stinks to high heaven. Black was his favourite colour and one of his most prized possessions was a leather jacket, although he also liked a shirt and tie. His hair was long while everyone else's was short and he'd paint his face with artificial sun tan lotion before anyone else had ever heard of it. He once saw a road sign saying: 'Danger! Cripples crossing' and laughed until he cried. He'd also be doubled up by comedians like The Goons and Peter Cook. When *That Was The Week That Was* came on the television he would either stay home to see it or leave a party early. Later when he moved up to London, he would write letters every day and they were always hilarious."

Syd's final year at The County was clouded by his father's sudden illness, which was eventually diagnosed as terminal cancer. He died that December, aged 52, having continued to work at Addenbrooke's – where he was pioneering research into what is now known as 'cot death syndrome' – until a fortnight before his final relapse.

Syd and Rosemary were devastated. "His father's death affected Roger a lot," says his sister. "You would never think they were close but they had a sort of unique closeness. If Rog said anything witty, our father would always be the first to laugh."

While not showing his grief openly, he did betray his feelings in one small way. Roger had religiously kept a diary from the age of 11, never missing a day. Some weeks later Rosemary saw that the entry for December 11 had been left blank. To Libby, Syd had simply said: "Poor dad died today."

Chapter Two

Leonard's Lodgers

N ow 16, Syd threw himself into the the teenage round of parties, cigarettes, booze and casual sex.

While art remained his main interest – he held an exhibition of his work in a local hall that spring – pop music ran a close second and encouraged by enthusiastic ovations at the Sunday afternoon get-togethers Syd joined his first band, Geoff Mott And The Mottoes.

Geoff Mott was a gangly, bespectacled, carrot-haired youth who had been expelled from The County for general unruliness prior to setting up his own rock 'n' roll band. Mott's rebellious image and comparative experience (he was 19, several years senior to the rest of the crowd) made him a minor celebrity among the town's fledgling rockers. He was the obvious frontman. Clive Welham was the drummer and 18-year-old Roger Waters, son of Syd's teacher Mary, was roped in on bass.

Waters was born in Great Bookham, Surrey, on September 9, 1943 (the year usually given is 1944). He was the second of two sons whose soldier father was killed in Anzio in 1944.

He had recently left school for a temporary job with a Swavesey architect prior to going to London's Regent Street Polytechnic to study architecture in September 1962.

At Cambridge High School he was regarded as a rather introverted loner whose competitive nature made him a useful athlete and star member of the rugby team. That winter saw him playing at fly-half for Old Cambridgians with Geoff Mott outside him on the wing.

Waters lacked Gilmour's inherent musical ability and neither was he a natural explorer like Barrett. Nevertheless he set about learning the bass guitar with an almost unnatural determination. He had received his first six-string acoustic guitar from a Swedish relative at the age of 14 and later took classical lessons. His mother was tone deaf and his school teachers apparently offered little encouragement.

"I was considered a complete twat at almost everything," Waters told *Q* magazine in August 1987. "Most of the teachers were absolute swines and the school was only concerned with university entrance. It was a real battery farm. I hated it."

Geoff Mott And The Mottoes were, like dozens of Cambridge groups, formed purely for fun and without pretensions of stardom. The band's history consists of a solitary gig at a CND meeting in a local hall, the type of occasion, admits Mott, where they could not put a foot wrong.

With their flamboyant leader at his exuberant best, The Mottoes doggedly ran through a string of Buddy Holly and Eddie Cochran numbers, spurred on by the generous applause of their captive audience.

"Syd wasn't a bad rhythm guitarist," says Mott. "It was nice to hear someone who could play as opposed to thumping around."

The Mottoes' CND triumph was never to be repeated, although they talked enthusiastically about another gig. Mott had a full-time job and was already in a semi-pro band, while Waters was on the verge of moving up to London.

Syd, for his part, found precious little in the 1962 music scene to inspire him. His favourite record was 'Green Onions' by Booker T And The MGs, the group of crack Memphis session musicians led by Steve Cropper who would go on to back many of the soul stars on Stax Records. He also liked the leading jazz trumpeter Miles Davis, an artist few of his contemporaries had even heard of.

In addition Syd raved about an unknown American singer he thought was called Bob Die Lon. He spent hours searching vainly for his records in local record stores. Only later did he learn the name was Bob Dylan.

"Syd was the year below me at Cambridge High," recalls Storm Thorgeson, who in the late sixties set up the hugely successful design company Hipgnosis which would design sleeves for countless top bands, Pink Floyd included. "At the time I came to know him he was heavily into girls. Sex and music were his big things when he was 16.

"The town was full of teenagers and we liked to think of ourselves as socially rebellious, though none of us really was. About the most rebellious thing we did was gatecrash parties. Most of the summer was spent sitting around on riverbanks with guitars and having picnics."

At last Syd's life was going the way he wanted. His oppressive schooldays behind him, he embarked on a two-year diploma at the Cambridge Technical College art department. The course began that September when one of Syd's fellow art students was his friend John Gordon.

If Barrett expected instant artistic liberation, he was in for a shock. While the art school set-up was considerably more relaxed than The County, it still had certain rules and regulations which were particularly frustrating for someone like Syd who felt his artistic development was being stunted by them.

"He was often misunderstood," says John Gordon. "People thought he was rebellious but the one thing he couldn't stand as an art student was time wasters. If we had a lecturer who was particularly boring he would become so disruptive that he would be thrown out of the class, if he hadn't walked out already.

"One time this chap arrived to give a lecture on a type of architectural moulding called egg and dart. He walked in without introducing himself and started writing on the blackboard. This boring old fart-type of lecturer really rankled Syd. He was always rather mature for his age and hated being treated like a child. He asked this chap his name but he evidently misheard and replied: 'Egg and dart.' Syd called him Mr Egg and Dart for the rest of the lesson and ended up making a mockery of the bloke."

Also in the class was a student called David Gilbert who would share a flat with Syd in Highgate in North London a couple of years later. "For reasons best known to himself," says Gilbert, "Syd launched into a quite brilliant imitation of a spastic, contorting his face into a series of bizarre shapes and constantly interrupting the lecture from the back of the class with cries of 'Scuse me Mr Egg and Dart.'

"His act was so convincing the lecturer didn't dare expel him because he couldn't be entirely sure that it wasn't for real. Syd only managed to get away with it by keeping it up throughout the entire lesson."

John Gordon adds: "Syd and I were as bad as each other. We used to bring our guitars to the Tech to entertain others and sometimes hid them under our desks to play them with our feet so the lecturer didn't know where the sound was coming from. We ended up getting that bloke the sack."

Storm Thorgeson grew up with Barrett and remembers him being impressed by a record called 'Love Me Do' by a northern group called The Beatles. "He grabbed my shoulder and said: 'Storm, man, this is it!' The effect was as immediate as that. The Beatles and Bo Diddley were his thing, while the rest of us were still into Elvis."

It is worth speculating, perhaps, what course Syd's life might have taken had he not been so gripped by the strains of The Beatles' début disc. He would probably have pursued a career in art, either as a lecturer or as a full-time artist. Instead he was besotted with the idea of becoming a pop star and threw himself into mastering the guitar. He would drag Libby along to the local youth club to watch the resident guitarist.

"He was totally lost," she remembers. "I used to loathe that guitar, like every girlfriend did. One minute we'd be getting ready to go out and he'd be saying he loved me and the next he'd find a new chord and concentrate on that for the rest of the evening."

It was later that year that Syd's old favourite Bob Dylan came to town during his first British tour and the 17-year-old Barrett, who by now had swapped his acoustic guitar for an electric, was among the first to buy tickets.

"My first reaction was seeing all these people like Syd," says Libby. "It was almost as if each town had sent one Syd Barrett there. It was the first time I'd seen people who were like him."

During the exciting summer of 1963 Libby's parents travelled to Greece for a holiday, leaving their daughter and her Beatle-mad boyfriend in the rather less exotic surroundings of a Butlins holiday camp in Essex.

The morning calls, forced holiday camp humour and cramped chalets – typical of Butlins' cheap family holiday style of the time – all appealed to Syd's sense of the ridiculous and Libby remembers him acting like The Beatles in *Help!* throughout their stay.

One night he took her out to Whittlesey to watch a London-based rhythm and blues group called The Rolling Stones. "It was around the time The Stones made 'Poison Ivy'. There weren't many people there, but Syd had heard of them and knew they were going to be great. God knows how. It was only a tiny village hall in Cambridgeshire."

Within minutes Mick Jagger had noticed the dark figure watching him from the back of the hall. When the interval came Libby, who had been ogling Jagger all the way through, was more than a bit miffed when the singer came over and introduced himself to Syd.

She was temporarily forgotten as the pair began a long discussion on musical trends over a couple of drinks. Syd also got talking to The Stones' lean, angular bass guitarist Bill Wyman who confessed he could hardly play the instrument and was still in the process of learning.

Barrett may have been a person of undoubted charisma and immense popularity, but occasionally he retreated deep into himself and would wander off into the hills near Cambridge or go for a solitary walk around the town's botanical gardens.

Another teenage friend Tim Francis says: "Syd was someone who, despite being very gregarious on the surface, had a very secret side. There was a part of him you could never reach."

As the new academic year started, he was joined at the Tech by Dave Gilmour who had left the claustrophobic Perse to study for 'A'-level examinations. Gilmour had blossomed into a fine guitarist, technically well ahead of Barrett, and the two of them spent many a lunchtime in one of the classrooms working their way through Stones' riffs.

John Gordon: "Syd and Dave were rivals in a friendly sort of way. Dave was always in a local band and Syd never got one together. Dave always enjoyed pointing out to Syd that he'd never formed a successful money-making band."

Goaded by these taunts, Syd briefly joined a student band that year. The outfit was called Those Without, a name inspired by a Françoise Sagan novel. Despite being received well at a number of gigs, it was clearly nothing more than a run-of-the-mill R&B band, certainly unable to compete on the same stage as Dave Gilmour and his band.

Cambridge was becoming too small for Syd anyway and that autumn he travelled up to London for an interview at Camberwell Art College in Peckham, borrowing a pair of Libby's father's shoes for the occasion. Unfortunately, the interview clashed with The Beatles' concert appearance at the Cambridge ABC cinema for which Syd had bought tickets months in advance.

"Syd loved John Lennon and it nearly killed him to have to miss that," says Libby.

The sacrifice was worthwhile, however, as he was told he could join the college on a three-year course in fine arts the following autumn. It was a long wait and in the interval Syd continued to paint.

By the spring of 1964, his friend John Gordon had noticed a distinct change in Syd's art as it became increasingly abstract. "He would dip old clothes in paint and stick them on a canvas . . . it became difficult to tell whether it was a painting or sculpture," he says.

Barrett arrived in London in the summer of 1964, at the same time as former High School colleague Bob Klose. At 19, Klose had built a reputation as a promising jazz guitarist with a Cambridge band called Blues Anonymous and was now to take architecture at Regent Street Polytechnic where Roger Waters had been studying for the last two years.

Waters had been living in a Highgate house recently vacated by fellow students Nick Mason and Rick Wright. Klose, Barrett and Dave Gilbert moved in. Barrett and Waters split a room between them while Klose shared with Gilbert.

Mason, whose wealthy family lived in an exclusive part of Hampstead, had temporarily moved back home. Wright, who was educated at the expensive Haberdashers School in south London, had just married Juliette Gale, lead singer with a defunct college group variously known at Sigma Six, The Screaming Abdabs or The Megadeaths.

The house was owned by a middle-aged architect called Mike Leonard who would occasionally employ Waters and Mason for part-time work. Leonard was by all accounts no ordinary landlord.

His attic was crammed with Chinese gongs, xylophones and oriental flutes and surprisingly, for someone in his late thirties, Leonard took a keen interest in the embryonic group formed by Klose, Barrett, Waters and Mason.

In fact he could hardly ignore them, as when the four were busy rehearsing in the basement the noise was so loud that Leonard's overhead office throbbed. "You could hear them when you turned off the main road a quarter of a mile away," says Mike Leonard. "The noise was phenomenal and although the neighbours sent round the police and council officials, the band didn't seem too worried. Then they had a lawyer's letter claiming someone's health was being damaged half a dozen houses away and threatening to sue them for invasion of privacy."

Far from lecturing his lodgers on the importance of neighbourly relations, Leonard actually encouraged them. After a few weeks Waters and Mason managed to cajole a couple of local pub landlords into letting them play a short set. Leonard sat in on organ.

"I didn't have the right image because I wasn't hairy and I was about 15 years older than the rest so people used to look at me rather suspiciously," he says.

Being the best musician, Klose played lead, supported by Waters on bass and Barrett on rhythm, while Mason tried to hold the whole thing together on drums.

His brief period in the spotlight over, Leonard reverted to being the band's roadie but he still had a vital role to play in the group's history.

"Mike was interested in light shows," says Bob Klose. "We were rehearsing at the Hornsey Art College one day when we saw him messing about with lights and putting patterns on a screen. At the time it didn't seem terribly important, but looking back that moment could be regarded as the beginning of Floyd's light shows."

The band called themselves, appropriately enough, Leonard's Lodgers.

They quickly drew up a rota with each member responsible for various domestic chores around the flat. Syd was in charge of cooking and after the lodgers decided they could live on one shilling each a day (five new pence), he produced a succession of appalling meals that consisted almost entirely of yellowing cabbage and Brussels sprouts. It was only later that they discovered Syd had been spending only a shilling a day on all four of them.

The boys would sit round a large table that had formerly been the kitchen door while Syd dished out his latest culinary atrocity amid mounting trepidation. Occasionally the feast would be interrupted by rows of tiny faces peering in at the window. The little girls of the neighbourhood had noticed their long hair and guitars and mistaken them for The Rolling Stones.

"They were a bunch of practical jokers," says Leonard. "On one occasion, one of Roger's friends brought round a large monkey which they chained to a tree to scare the life out of the neighbours. I remember Syd as someone with a sense of humour and I can still hear his particular chuckle.

"From the beginning he was writing his own whimsical songs, although I don't know if any of those originals got on record."

What the band lacked most was a frontman. Highgate's answer to The Stones had no Mick Jagger, and none of them fancied handling the lead vocals. Further recruitment was required. After a couple of months the ranks were increased when Rick Wright was brought in on piano but the focal problem remained.

Syd decided to search back home in Cambridge and called in at Geoff Mott's flat to see if he fancied coming up to London. At the time Mott's pop prospects were considerably brighter than Syd's. A year earlier he had formed an R&B band called The Boston Crabs who had built up a large following in Cambridge and were destined to have a brief stab at the national charts the following year. It is no surprise that the response to Syd's offer was far from enthusiastic.

Mott was settled in Cambridge, had a good job and was getting £30 a week from band work. What did he want to hike up to London for and play in an unknown group? He made what seemed the sensible decision at the time but in later years was inclined to torture himself with the thought of what might have been had he accepted the offer.

"I seem to have had a lifetime of people saying: 'If only you'd joined Leonard's Lodgers'," he says. "But the stuff they went on to do was vastly different to mine and we'd have gone our own ways eventually – that thought is the one thing that keeps me sane."

Although Geoff Mott didn't want the job, someone else did. At least temporarily.

In a West End music store, Klose and Waters stumbled across a tall blues singer they vaguely knew from Cambridge. Royal Air Force junior technician Chris Dennis was a bit long in the tooth at 26 but he had been a member of the well-known Cambridge band The Redcaps and, more importantly, he had a large repertoire of blues material. Dennis was looking for a band, The Lodgers needed a singer, so they got together.

Syd's Cambridge trip had failed to unearth a singer, but he did return with a new name for the band. As he patiently explained to Bob Klose, he had a couple of records by two grizzled Georgia bluesmen named Pink Anderson and Floyd Council. How about putting the two Christian names together? The boys had managed to buy a battered Bedford van with money from their student grants. Syd painted their new name Pink Floyd in bright pink letters over the black wheel arch.

Later, he would often claim that the peculiar name was transmitted to him from an overhead flying saucer while he was sitting on the ley line crossing Glastonbury Tor in Somerset.

The Pink Floyd that Chris Dennis joined that autumn was probably not as proficient as the band he had left back in Cambridge. "Bob Klose was a pretty good guitarist and the only real musician in the band," he says. "But even at this stage Syd had a few eccentric ideas.

"The guy who owned the house was another eccentric and used to make advertising jingles for television. He had these gongs and electronic devices in the attic and Syd used to experiment with the various noises. I guess that was how he worked out the early Floyd sound.

"But at this stage we were like a lot of other bands, doing R&B stuff. Syd did a lot of Bo Diddley numbers on his white Fender guitar. He'd do 'No Money Down' and I would sing Jimmy Witherspoon, Muddy Waters and Chuck Berry stuff along with Lazy Lester's 'I'm A Lover Not A Fighter' and 'I Got Love If You Want It' by Slim Harpo."

The new line-up made its début at a private party in a well-to-do house in Surrey and went on to play at a couple of polytechnics, as well as the Beat City Club in Oxford Street, before Dennis was posted to the Persian Gulf in January 1965.

For the next 18 months Pink Floyd was to remain little more than a hobby. Waters, Mason, Wright and Klose had no intention of giving up their studies, while Barrett was still absorbed in his painting.

Syd had enjoyed his first term at Camberwell, where his abstract art had won the approval of his tutor, Chris 'Chimp' Chamberlain. Barrett proved an eager young purist, ready to argue the merits of using one brush – a technique he felt carried more integrity as the strokes were all the same size.

Most of his paintings were of flowers, although he would occasionally come up with a human portrait. When Sandie Shaw hit number one with 'There's Always Something There To Remind Me' in October 1964, Syd painted her portrait. He sent it to her press office only to be bitterly disappointed when he got no reply.

Chamberlain saw considerable artistic talent in Barrett but realised he was being drawn away by his interest in music. In his second year at Camberwell, Syd reached a crossroads. Exciting as college life was, the harsh fact was that unless an art student showed exceptional promise, the only career he could pursue at the end of the three-year course was teaching.

The thought of a return to the classroom was intolerable. It forced Barrett to seek other outlets for his artistic talents. His role in the group became increasingly important and he developed confidence handling lead vocals and in his own songs. The amusing 'Effervescing Elephant' had been written while lazing on the banks of the River Cam a few years earlier. Now he came up with two other songs, 'Flutter By Butterfly' and 'Bike', the latter allegedly inspired by a large Raleigh bicycle belonging to his new Cambridge girlfriend Jenny Spires (later to feature in another Barrett song 'Lucifer Sam') although she has since dismissed the connection as "a load of rubbish."

Floyd continued to play the usual round of parties, pubs and polytechnics, once even appearing at Homerton College in Hills Road, Cambridge, on the same night that Geoff Mott's Boston Crabs supported the chart-topping Unit Four Plus Two.

By the spring, however, it was clear that a rift was developing within the ranks. Bob Klose, who was not helped by a rather introverted personality, favoured a more traditional jazz approach and began finding himself increasingly at odds with Syd who was heavily into The Stones, mysticism and sex.

"Bob was a good guitarist but the others were getting a bit uneasy about his playing," says Dave Gilbert. "His style was neither relaxed nor comfortable. He used to stand there screwing his face up and the others would say: 'Come on Bob how about acting more like a pop star?'"

As the end of the summer term loomed, it was clear that Klose's days in the group were numbered. Moreover, he was apparently under pressure to quit from his parents who felt his pop career was blossoming at the expense of his architectural studies.

Klose officially left the group at the start of the summer holidays, conceding that he and the others were moving in different musical directions. It was an amicable parting and he would sometimes get up on stage and jam with them the following term. He remembers Barrett as someone of undoubted talent.

"He had almost too much talent, if such a thing is possible. And also this strange charisma. But there were definitely no signs of what was to come. He was tremendously gifted and seemed more interested in painting. With hindsight that's what he should have stuck to. The music business is so full of cheats and exploiters that a true artist is always going to be vulnerable."

Chapter Three

An Orange, A Plum And A Matchbox

T he summer of 1965 saw the beginning of Syd Barrett's voyage of self-discovery. Back in Cambridge during the summer vacation, he and Storm Thorgeson became interested in Sant Mat, an offshoot Sikh sect. Storm passed his interview and was initiated by the Mantra, but Syd was turned away for being too young. He was crushingly disappointed.

"Syd was always very involved in things," says Thorgeson. "He embraced this religious cause, his painting and his dress sense, with a terrific degree of enthusiasm."

That August, Syd and a few others set out for southern France in a Land Rover. Dave Gilmour, who had already hitched down to St Tropez, was taking a break from his newly-formed band Jokers Wild. They had attracted national attention when one of its members was caught with a girl in his bedroom at a student hall of residence.

While Syd was away in London, Gilmour had been enjoying the life of a minor celebrity as a freelance guitarist in Cambridge. His playing had improved to the point where he was often hired by local bands, and he was able to charge far more than the band was actually paid for the night's show. His reputation was such that they always paid up without a murmur.

St Tropez did not take kindly to the impoverished Cambridge buskers. Barrett, Gilmour and company were arrested and whisked off for questioning at the local police station.

After an hour, the police found nothing and had no reason to hold the young musicians. They were fortunate as that summer the Cambridge set were already experimenting heavily with the drug that the name Pink Floyd was to become synonymous with – Lysergic Acid Diethylamide, more commonly known as LSD.

When Storm Thorgeson was considering an album cover for the 1974 album bringing together Barrett's two solo LPs, he wanted something that was 'typically Syd'. When the collection was released that September, it showed a stark, black and white picture of Syd sitting cross-legged on the painted floorboards of his Earls Court Square flat in 1969. The picture was set on a simple fawn-coloured background accompanied mysteriously by an orange, a plum and a matchbox.

The joke was lost on all but Barrett's closest friends who had joined in his early experimentation with drugs. "It arose out of his first acid trip in the garden of a friend called Dave Gale who lived in Cambridge," says Thorgeson. "When you are on acid your attention focuses on one thing. Syd happened to pick up these three objects and kept them with him for about 12 hours, telling us how amazing they were. He'd carry them around with him and hoard them in a corner."

Long-time Floyd associate Ian Moore, known as Imo to the band and their friends, describes the farcical events that led up to the incident. The participants of course were completely naïve about the possible dangers of the drug they were toying with.

"We got hold of some liquid LSD in bottles, laid out hundreds of sugar cubes in rows and put two drops on each. But the stuff was so strong we were absorbing it through our fingers, or more likely by licking it off them. As it took effect we had no idea which cubes we had done, so many of them probably got double doses while the rest did not have any. Syd had his plum, orange and matchbox and was sitting staring at them during his trip. Whatever he was into was his whole world – to him the plum was the planet Venus and the orange was Jupiter. Syd was floating in space between them."

His interstellar travels ended abruptly when Moore, on another trip altogether, took a liking to the plum and ate Syd's Venus in a mouthful. "You should have seen Syd's face. He was in total shock for a few seconds, then he just grinned."

Syd was 19 when he experienced this first acid trip but he had been smoking marijuana for at least two years before that, first taking it during the Sunday afternoon sessions at Hills Road. He was heavily into experimentation, and though he had tried heroin by the time he was 20, LSD would always remain his favourite form of escape.

That Barrett eventually came to rely on the drug and show inexplicably violent moods, is hardly surprising in the light of later LSD research which showed that during the first few hours after taking it there were often outbreaks of uncontrollable violent behaviour – something many of Barrett's friends and future lovers were to find out.

LSD first became front page news in Britain in 1965 as a result of teenagers using 'morning glory' seeds found to contain small quantities of LSD. The pure drug used in experiments by Barrett and his friends was many times more concentrated.

Moore recalls how the Cambridge crowd persuaded a friend to smuggle a large consignment of marijuana back from Morocco in the boot of his car. The man, who genuinely didn't know what they wanted it for, sold it to them for £2 a pound. Once more the group experimented with abandon.

"We did practically everything," says Moore. "We smoked it, made tea with it, ate it. You name it, we did it. Dope was everywhere in Cambridge. When I lived with a mate in Clarendon Street, there was a period when we didn't go out of the flat for three months. We stayed in that smoke-filled flat, living on nothing and hardly eating."

Driven by hunger, they would periodically descend on Storm Thorgeson's house. Storm's parents had split up and he lived with his mother, a notoriously light sleeper. "We had to be ever so quiet because his mother would hear everything," says Moore. "If we had toast, even the sound of the toaster popping up would wake her. Syd and the rest of us would be upstairs smoking dope until three in the morning, which made us incredibly hungry. We would go down and make huge cheese sandwiches with marmalade – ridiculous feasts whenever we had these crazy urges. The cornflakes were a problem though – they made so much noise."

When someone discovered a London LSD supplier, the really riotous behaviour began. Whenever someone's parents were away, the group would take over the vacant house, away from prying eyes. "None of the parents knew what was going on," says Moore. "Syd's mother was very liberal-minded and put his behaviour down to youthful high spirits. Anyone on dope or acid looks perfectly normal. The only giveaway is those heavily dilated pupils and overpowering direct eye contact. You are the only one who really sees things differently.

"Having no rules was something Syd had a thing about. He was well ahead of the things we were into because of his art and education. We were mainly into visuals but he went much further because of his intellectual side. He was for anarchy and rebellion. The pressures and the rules were screwing him up even then. Once, when Syd was on another trip in Dave Gale's garden, he kept going into the house, back into the garden and then into the house again. Eventually he and another bloke ended up in the bath together, jumping up and down shouting: 'No rules! No rules!' They really thought they had transcended all rules. Poor Dave Gale was going paranoid. He thought the bath was going to fall through the floor, but by then everyone was in hysterics and everything seemed funny."

Storm Thorgeson would occasionally take his acid-crazed friends into the countryside and shoot home-movies of their pathetic attempts to play football, or more avant-garde scenes with everyone upside down or naked. One film called *The Meal* centred around a picnic in which the guests ended up eating one of their fellow diners.

In 1985 the authors were shown an extraordinary home movie purporting to show one of Barrett's early acid trips. The colour film was shot by one of Syd's Cambridge friends, Nigel Lesmoire-Gordon in a disused quarry and features the 19-year-old Barrett clad in an all-black outfit which pre-empts the so-called Gothic look of today's generation by 25 years.

The film comes into focus to reveal Barrett's unmistakable figure pointing somewhat menacingly at the distant hand-held camera. He then races to the steep quarry face which he proceeds to scale with the agility of a mountain goat. Not content with this piece of youthful bravado Syd then begins a reckless charge around the rim of the precipice pausing only briefly to peer down at the cameraman in the quarry below.

The surreal sequence ends with Syd gazing in disbelief at his fingers which appear to sprout mushrooms before his very eyes. The last shot is a bizarre close-up of Syd's face with mushrooms where his eyes should be. Lesmoire-Gordon today makes his living as a film editor and this film obviously represents an early stab at the avant-garde with Syd relishing his role in the spotlight.

During Syd's second year at Camberwell the band carried on much the same as before. The members still couldn't decide on a name, sometimes appearing as The Pink Floyd Sound. By November, when they returned to Cambridge for the social event of the year, they were calling themselves The T-Set.

The event was the 21st birthday party of Storm Thorgeson's girlfriend, an occasion that brought together Pink Floyd and Dave Gilmour's Jokers Wild for the first time.

Storm's girlfriend, Libby January, was from a wealthy Cambridge family. Her parents had laid on a magnificent party but the strait-laced Januarys didn't really know what they were letting themselves in for by inviting some of their daughter's 'hip' friends.

The stage was set for a grand coming-of-age celebration in classic Cambridge débutante style. There was a marquee on the lawn with the whole January family assembled alongside their society guests. But it was on the two-foot high band stand that the real action was happening.

Dave Gilmour remembers that an unknown young American singer-guitarist called Paul Simon was also booked to appear, and the three acts took it in turns to perform their songs. "My band backed Paul Simon playing Chuck Berry stuff like 'Johnny B. Goode'," he recalls.

Another Cambridge friend, Pip Carter, who would become the Floyd's lighting man the following year, joined Jokers Wild on the bongos for their version of The Beatles' 'Michelle', while Moore got in on the act by singing a Bo Diddley song with Syd.

Later on, Roger Waters, Nick Mason, Rick Wright and Syd were joined on stage by Gilmour, filling out The T-Set sound. "It was strange that Syd and Dave's bands played together at that stage," says Carter. "It was the first time they were all up together."

Mr January was a member of the old school who would make everyone stand to attention whenever the Queen appeared on television. It isn't difficult to imagine how he reacted when the party mood got the better of his daughter's friends and they decided to liven up the evening.

"It was a total division between straights and non-straights," says Storm Thorgeson. "We all got so dreadfully smashed we had to be carried out while everyone else stood around in their suits. God knows what Paul Simon made of it all."

"There was a bunch of young farmer types at one end of the tent with all the rich people, and the rest of us were at the other," recalls Ian Moore. "It was as though there were two separate parties and it was obvious something would happen.

"Syd was the one to start things off. He grabbed a tablecloth and called for everyone to watch as he did his famous glasses trick. He yanked the cloth away, but instead of staying on the table the glasses flew everywhere."

At the other end of the tent Mr January paled visibly and his wife was seen to clutch her brow and mutter: "Oh my God!"

Worse was to follow as Syd stumbled on stage again, bottle of gin in hand, for an unscheduled encore with Moore. Mercifully they fell off the stage before reaching the microphone.

By some miracle, the night actually ended well for Storm Thorgeson, who was given permission to take Libby's hand in marriage.

Over the next few months, Syd's original name – Pink Floyd – came back into favour and his experimental ideas became increasingly influential. More importantly, the group were making subtle transitions in their repertoire and delivery and, although still playing covers of R&B standards, slowly but surely were developing a sound of their own.

In February 1966, they made their début at The Marquee Club in London's Wardour Street at an event which came to be known as *The Spontaneous Underground*.

The invitations read: "Who will be there? Poets, pop singers, hoods, Americans, homosexuals (because they make up 10 per cent of the population), 20 clowns, jazz musicians, one murderer, sculptors, politicians and some girls who defy description, are among those invited."

The audience organised its own entertainment. Donovan, in red Cleopatra makeup, made up songs on the spot to backing from six sitars and a conga drum. Then a girl in white tights played a Bach Prelude and Fugue while The Ginger Johnson African Drummers pounded out furious rhythms all around her.

But the loudest and most outrageous of all were Pink Floyd who played lengthy, muffled versions of 'Roadrunner' and Chuck Berry songs, or simply built up layer upon layer of feedback by turning everything up to full volume.

Among the baffled onlookers that day was Peter Jenner, who with his partner Andrew King had lately launched an ambitious and somewhat 'alternative' pop management company called Blackhill Enterprises. He was intrigued by this strange but highly original sound.

Jenner, a teacher at the London School of Economics, was on the look-out for a psychedelic group to sign to producer Joe Boyd's London branch of Elektra Records. His partner Andrew King, on the other hand, was not the slightest bit interested in pop but had reached the conclusion that "the best way to become rich and trendy was to manage a rock group." Clearly Pink Floyd fitted the bill as a far-out freaky electronic pop group.

According to Jenner, when he first saw Floyd they were on the point of breaking up due to low morale and lack of gigs. He tracked them down to their Highgate flat and was astonished to discover their amateur set-up – no contracts, no agency, no management – and that the gear they used was either home-made or in imminent danger of falling apart. Even so, Jenner rashly said he could make the group "bigger than The Beatles" – the traditional boast of any aspiring manager to this day – and immediately contacted his partner.

King duly resigned from his job as an educational cyberneti-cist (even he is unclear quite what it meant) and agreed to take on a group of apparent no-hopers that he had never seen and who were just about to clear off on their summer holidays.

By this time Syd had actually left the Highgate flat for a Bohemian existence in a whole series of student hang-outs, finally joining a crowd of Cambridge hipsters at a house in Kensington's Cromwell Road where LSD was distributed freely. He played two records endlessly that summer – The Byrds' 'Fifth Dimension' and Love's début album. He would later develop a riff from Love's 'My Little Red Book' for his own 'Interstellar Overdrive'.

Syd had also begun a two-year relationship with a blonde Cambridge girl called Lynsey Korner who had moved to London to work as a part-time model. After a few months at the chaotic Cromwell Road flat, where Yoko Ono reputedly filmed her celebrated *Bottoms* movie, they moved to a flat near Egerton Court. Barrett was still painting but his work was now heavily influenced by his sparkling acid-driven visions. In the new flat hung a painting of a man's head with a train coming through the forehead. Underneath someone had printed the words: 'That's weird.'

When Pink Floyd played at the opening of the Chalk Farm Roundhouse on October 11, Jenner and King brought in a Heath Robinson lighting machine built from British Home Stores light switches and domestic light bulbs which shone through coloured Perspex pinned to a makeshift wooden frame. Pip Carter – another casualty of the Cambridge drug scene – was called upon to operate the flimsy rig. The Roundhouse was the biggest gig Floyd had played to date and the event brought all factions of the emergent underground scene under the same roof for the first time. Over 2,500 people squeezed in and many more failed to get through the doors.

The new venue had stood empty for more than a decade. It was built as an engine shed, then used to store giant vats of gin. It had never been used as an entertainment venue and was absolutely filthy. It was also freezing cold, but people had queued outside for hours. The steep stairs were so narrow that the audience could only enter in small groups and many did not get in until after 2.30am.

Once inside, other hardships followed. The 2,500 punters were expected to share two toilets. These quickly overflowed and the doors were ripped off to be used as duck boards.

Paul McCartney came dressed as an Arab in white robes and headdress, arriving in a duffle coat to disguise himself. He needn't have bothered – no one paid much attention to him or his girlfriend, Jane Asher. They simply merged into the throng.

Marianne Faithful won the Shortest and Barest Prize for her nun's habit which *New Society* described as "not quite reaching the ground." In fact it didn't even cover her bottom.

Another Floyd associate, actor Matthew Scurlow, believes the event, and particularly Barrett's part in it, had a profound effect on McCartney and contributed to The Beatles' 'Sgt. Pepper' album.

A mountain of jelly was to be handed out to the audience but before a note had been played Syd and Pip Carter, looking for a piece of wood to repair the temperamental Jenner-King light-show, spotted part of the structure designed to support the mould. They tugged and a 17-foot wall of jelly crashed down giving their Chelsea clothes an unexpected splash of additional colour.

"The Floyd were playing mad interpretations of well-known songs – psychedelic blues such as 'Cops And Robbers' with Syd improvising like hell," says Pip Carter. "He was using his Zippo (a metal cigarette lighter) on his guitar as well as running ball bearings down the neck to produce controlled feedback. Some of Syd's tunings came from playing the blues, but most came straight out of his head."

Floyd's light show was well received and despite blowing out the power midway through 'Interstellar Overdrive', they had been noticed. National press coverage of the event did much to increase attendances at subsequent gigs.

On October 31, Barrett, Waters, Mason and Wright signed a six-way contract with Jenner and King and became part of the Blackhill Publishing company. King had taken the name from the Welsh border cottage he owned.

"Syd later stayed in it a few times, wrote a few songs there and used to hang out with his dodgy friends. It became quite notorious and eventually the local police nearly closed it as a disorderly house," he says.

Soon after, Jenner and King pushed the group into recording some demo tapes at The Thompson Private Recording Studio in Hemel Hempstead. They chose 'I Get Stoned' – one of Syd's first serious songwriting efforts – and 'Let's Roll Another One'. The latter eventually saw the light of day as 'Candy And A Currant Bun' on the B-side of their first single.

'Sitting here all alone, I get stoned,' Syd had written on 'I Get Stoned'. The words were pathetically prophetic.

King maintains that the quality of the recordings was quite good – "similar to things people do on home portastudios today" – but Floyd's first attempt to woo the record companies flopped. Years later, King and the studio owners waged a bitter legal battle for the rights to the tapes.

Jenner's prime target Joe Boyd heard the two songs and advised the group to spend more money on professional tapes.

In December the Floyd played at the first *Night Tripper* event at The Blarney Club in Tottenham Court Road. The advertisement, in issue five of the underground magazine *IT* (*International Times*) gave no indication who would be playing, but Floyd had been invited to appear and the audience knew by word of mouth who they were turning up to see. A week later the Friday night-only gathering changed its name to UFO, the legendary first underground club of the psychedelic era.

"At the first two or three UFO's, the Floyd were on 60 per cent of the gross to provide music and lights," says Jenner. "My first managerial blunder was allowing that to be altered to straight bread instead of a percentage because the place instantly became very fashionable. I've never seen anything like it since."

"Occasionally a drunk who normally only went down there on regular nights would stagger in and be confronted by this vision like Dante's Inferno," says Pip Carter. "The audience would sit, lie or shag. It was totally over the top. Anything went."

Miles of *IT* wrote: "To open the doors to the big basement room was a big shock. The damp heat hit you in the face like a gorilla's breath. The pulsating bubbles of the light show crawled over the walls, the ceiling and the floor. The reek of incense cut across the acrid aroma of hash and sweat."

Rock journalist Hugh Fielder was a Cambridge contemporary of the Floyd. He had once played in a band called The Rambling Blues which had made the costly mistake of hiring Dave Gilmour for a gig and were then horrified to find out how much he charged. When Fielder left Cambridge for a business studies course at the West London Polytechnic, he decided to check out Floyd at UFO.

"No one ever knew whether UFO stood for Unidentified Flying Object or Underground Freak-Out," he says. "We went along and thought the Floyd were rubbish. What was this noise? There was no R&B and it seemed to have no form at all. We thought it was ludicrous. Then we went back to see them with Procol Harum a couple of weeks later and it suddenly clicked. There was a definite feeling that you were in on something. It was only a question of getting on the right wavelength. Once you were, you could connect with anything they were doing musically.

"Syd was fascinating. He seemed to spend most of his time with his back to the audience, detuning his guitar, which was astonishing. You could see the rest of the band struggling to keep up. Syd was already experimenting and it only worked half the time. It all revolved around him. The rest of the band could only follow. The others had discipline, particularly Nick and Roger. Rick was good at filling in while Syd occasionally sat cross-legged on the stage playing with himself mentally and physically. They were never a particularly communicative band on stage but they had their set fairly well worked out and just went ahead with it.''

UFO became the focus of the underground. It was to Pink Floyd what The Cavern had been to The Beatles and, in fact, was one of the few places where the Fab Four could walk around relatively unmolested.

The Who's guitarist Pete Townshend went to see Procol Harum on the night 'A Whiter Shade Of Pale' was released and again when it was at number two in the charts. He often paid many times the normal 10 shillings (50 pence) fee, knowing that *International Times*, which financed the club, was in danger of folding through lack of money. Townshend has fond memories of UFO.

''When the Floyd played it was very exciting. Their sound fitted that period with echo on all the instruments. I once got Eric Clapton to come down because I thought what Syd was doing was very interesting. We both enjoyed him, although you could never quite hear what he was up to because he used two or three different echo units in a row. He used to have them coming out of different amps which formed a kind of sound field – a textural wash of sound that wasn't always melodically or harmonically correct but always very interesting and satisfying.''

Hugh Fielder: ''I came across Jimi Hendrix in the loo once. He was wearing trousers with no flies and yes, it was enormous. I can confirm all the rumours are true . . .

''The Floyd were never considered stars but were very much part of the London underground. Everyone was too laid back to scream. We used to stagger out of the club at six am and take the first tube home, sitting there in our kaftans and beads among the early morning commuters.

''Outside London it was a different story. They would sometimes be bottled off stage. They rather restricted themselves by not compromising.''

Pink Floyd's first venture out of the capital was to Canterbury Technical College, 60 miles away, on November 19. The reviewer from the local Canterbury newspaper was more liberal than most and wrote: ''The opening curtains revealed the group on stage wearing neutral shirts to reflect the coloured lights and standing in semi-darkness. Behind them was a 15-foot Buddha. On either side, sets of filtered spots sprayed various colours over the stage while modern art slides were projected behind.

"This weird conglomeration of sight and sound added up to a strange result. Those watching were a little mystified at first, but after the first rather frightening discordant notes (they) soon began dancing and gradually relaxed. It was an enjoyable if somewhat odd evening."

Rick Wright tried to explain the show. "It's completely spontaneous. We just turn up the amplifiers and develop it from there. But we still have a long way to go to get exactly what we want. It must develop still further.

"There is probably more co-ordination between us than any other pop group. We play more like a jazz group. We have come to think musically together when we're on stage."

There were, as Syd had often proclaimed: "No rules!"

The night before Canterbury, Floyd had taken their show to Hornsey College of Art, a more critical audience than usual. Seventeen-year-old Joe Gannon was helping out with the lights and had designed new slides for them. Gannon had ambitious ideas to replace the coloured slides projected onto the bare wall behind the group with moving film.

Hornsey was an important milestone for Floyd – the first of many gigs with a title: *Philadelic Music For Simian Hominids*.

On December 3, they played the *Psychedelia Versus Ian Smith* concert at The Roundhouse, organised for The Majority Rule For Rhodesia Committee. On December 12, they performed at the Royal Albert Hall and 10 days later they played The Marquee for the first time since Spontaneous Underground had launched a new era. A wind of change was storming through the pop scene and Pink Floyd, virtually unknown a couple of months earlier, were in the vanguard, landing a residency at The Marquee while still only a semi-pro outfit of albeit increasingly part-time students.

While the UFO all-nighters will always be linked with Pink Floyd's rise, the Marquee gigs finished in time for the tube home. Fancy-free young things with no parental control could enjoy a whole night at UFO, but The Marquee gave the group a far wider audience to spread the news.

The band had dropped most of their R&B material on the insistence of Jenner who impressed on them the need for more original songs of a 'weird' nature. Syd gladly complied, unaware that the hit single which would propel him to stardom was just around the corner.

Chapter Four

Is There Anybody In There?

1967, the 'Year Of Love', opened with the establishment receiving a series of shock waves from the underground. The Royal Institute For The Deaf issued a warning in *The Daily Mail* about the 120 decibels measured directly in front of the Floyd's speakers at UFO, claiming that hearing would be affected, while *The News Of The World* carried a two-part series on 'The Psychedelic Experience: Pop Stars and Drugs', which cast a critical eye on Floyd's 'LSD-inspired' light shows.

The revelations of reporter Mike Gabbert (who would himself attract notoriety as editor of the downmarket *Star* newspaper 20 years later) led indirectly to a police drugs raid on The Rolling Stones and the picketing of *The News Of The World* offices by members of UFO in retaliation.

Working on the old adage that any publicity is good publicity, Jenner and King must have been delighted at the way things were going. On February 1, Pink Floyd turned professional and just 27 days later entered Sound Techniques Studio in Chelsea to record their first single. The group planned to record six songs and pick the best two as the A and B-sides of the single.

Elektra boss Joe Boyd, who was the resident DJ at UFO, was a natural choice as producer. He knew the group personally, knew the sound they wanted, as well as what the underground expected of their 'house band'. Above all he had the cash to produce it.

With John Wood engineering, Floyd cut the Barrett songs 'Arnold Layne' and 'Let's Roll Another', which was renamed 'Candy And A Currant Bun' to make it more digestible for record companies and radio play.

Syd "became a bit flustered" when told his reference to dope smoking had to be cut out but Waters told him curtly to shut up. Waters disapproved of dope smoking in the studio, while Syd was naturally all for it. He often told friends that his fellow band members were "dead straight."

This clash of attitudes would later play a major part in Syd's departure, but for now everyone was so impressed by the chosen A-side, 'Arnold Layne', that Jenner and King decided to sell it to the highest bidder. Hardly surprising perhaps, for Floyd's début single remains one of their finest.

That said, it wasn't exactly what the group had planned. "In fact, we didn't want 'Arnold Layne' to be the first single," says Nick Mason. "We were asked to record six numbers then find a record company that would accept them. We recorded the first two and they were snatched from us. We were told that was it. All the record companies wanted the disc, so it was just a case of holding out for the biggest offer.

"We knew we wanted to be rock 'n' roll stars and we wanted to make singles, so it seemed the most suitable song to condense into three minutes without losing too much."

"From the word go they were four not terribly competent musicians who managed between them to create something that was extraordinary," says Jenner. "Syd was the main creative drive behind the band – he was the singer and lead guitarist. Roger couldn't tune his bass because he was tone deaf, it had to be tuned by Rick. Rick could write a bit of a tune and Roger could knock out a couple of words if necessary. 'Set The Controls For The Heart Of The Sun' on the second album was the first song Roger wrote, and he only did it because Syd encouraged everyone to write. Syd was very hesitant about his writing, but when he produced these great songs everyone else thought: 'Well, it must be easy . . .'."

Despite this initial hesitancy, Barrett produced a pop classic still played regularly, 20 years on, by all manner of radio DJs.

"Syd was certainly the first guitarist I knew to use a gadget called the Binson Echorette, which was a sort of predecessor to all the digital delay (echo) systems people use nowadays," says Andrew King. "It was a more complex version of the Watkins Copycat, which everyone later used. This was an upmarket version based on hardware originally built in the British Post

Office for recorded messages. It was a solid lump of metal with a recording head all the way round the outside. As the tape moved round and passed different heads it produced different echo effects. Syd used it on his guitar and no one had thought of it before."

Apart from the two single cuts, Floyd also recorded a version of 'Interstellar Overdrive' with Boyd which has never been released. Other planned songs had to wait as the band discovered that the 'psychedelia' coverage in the national press had made them a much sought after commodity.

Following an initial approach by Polydor, Floyd finally signed with EMI for a £5,000 advance. The image-conscious label was still not sure whether they had grabbed a tiger by the tail and issued a reassuring press release insisting that Pink Floyd did not know what people meant by Psychedelic Pop and were not trying to create hallucinatory effects for their audience. The rather laughable tactic failed miserably. When the single was released on March 11, it caused a sensation. Radio London immediately banned it, while the other pirate station apparently demanded too much payola.

'Arnold Layne' was a true story from the group's Cambridge days. "Both my mother and Syd's had students as lodgers because there was a girls' college up the road," says Waters. "So there were constantly great lines of bras and knickers on our washing lines. Arnold, or whoever he was, took bits and pieces off the washing lines."

Soon after the single's release, the British music paper *Melody Maker* sent Nick Jones to interview Syd at the flat he shared with Lynsey.

"Syd Barrett tumbled out of bed and donned his socks," wrote Jones. "I peeked round the small attic room, looking for women's clothing that Pink Floyd say Arnold tries on in front of his mirror. 'Syd, why did you write such a dirty, filthy, smutty, immoral and degrading song as Arnold Layne?' Syd blinked blankly: 'Well, I just wrote it. I thought Arnold Layne was a nice name and it fitted very well into the music I had already composed.'

"'But isn't it true,' said I, 'that Radio London quite rightly banned the record because they thought it was smutty?' Instead of reeling into the wardrobe and revealing a cupboard full of feminine clobber, Syd began to explain: 'I was in Cambridge at the time I started writing the song. I pinched the line about 'moonshine washing line' from Rog, our bass guitarist – because he has an enormous washing line in the back garden of his house. Then I thought Arnold must have a hobby, and it went from there.

"'Arnold Layne just happens to dig dressing up in women's clothing. A lot of people do, so let's face up to reality. About the only other lyric anybody could object to is the bit 'it takes two to know' – and there's nothing smutty about that!'"

The rest of the band also put in an appearance and ended up dragging Jones down to the pub for a few pints of "good old-fashioned brown beer." The *Melody Maker* writer, who seems to have been prepared for a drug-crazed orgy, was both surprised and relieved. Pink Floyd, he concluded lamely, were very ordinary people.

A more liberal stance was adopted by David Paul of *The Morning Star*, who felt 'Arnold Layne' was "clever and ironic." "It might seem an odd theme but that's because lyric writers are such a conservative lot," he wrote. "There's nothing sick or sensational about it and it makes a human change from endless love lyrics."

Waters told the press that he was upset by the press describing the single as smutty. "It's a real song about a real subject. It isn't just a collection of words like 'love', 'baby' or 'dig' put to music like the average pop song."

Melody Maker declared that Floyd had produced a good commercial single: "It takes a lot of plays to get tuned into, but without doubt they have come up with a good disc," wrote their reviewer. "The Pink Floyd represent a new form of music to the English pop scene, so let's hope the English are broad-minded enough to accept it with open arms."

It seemed the great British record-buying public was – though only to the extent of putting it straight into the April 22 *Record Mirror* chart at 20 before it dropped out again the next week. *New Musical Express* raved: "Off-beat weird lyric and blockbusting sound. Great organ work, twangs and spine chilling build. With all their publicity this could well be a hit."

Strange that the *NME* should pick up on Wright's organ playing as it seemed to the rest of the band that he was always playing the same riff, which they dubbed: "Rick's Fry's Turkish Delight Lick!" after the advert on British television.

Even the ultra-critical Scott Walker voted 'Arnold Layne' a hit in the *Melody Maker's* 'Blind Date' spot, where stars judged the weekly releases without knowing who was behind the sound. After savaging Sandie Shaw's 'Puppet On A String', saying, "It'll lose the Eurovision Song Contest definitely" (it eventually won), the chief Walker Brother confessed a liking for the Floyd's début disc, though he didn't recognise the group.

"It's different and the lyrics are interesting. It's about a transvestite? I haven't tried transvestism yet," he commented.

Syd's sister, Rosemary, now a trainee nurse living in Terrapin Road, Tooting (Barrett would later use the street name for one of his best-loved tracks on 'The Madcap Laughs') heard the record and wrote to say how much she liked it. Syd replied with a cheery note saying it was just the beginning.

Another who felt Floyd were destined for great things was the avant-garde poet-musician Pete Brown, who was writing songs with Cream bassist Jack Bruce at the time. He felt 'Arnold Layne' was a milestone in pop.

"Syd was one of the first people to get hits with poetry-type lyrics. The first time I heard 'Arnold Layne' I thought 'Fucking hell!' It was the first truly English song about English life with a tremendous lyric. It certainly unlocked doors and made things possible that up to that point no one thought were."

Another view is that Syd was writing in the shadow of his greatest influence, The Beatles. Their 'Eleanor Rigby' had topped the charts in September 1966 and 'Penny Lane' was at number two even as 'Arnold Layne' was released – both very English songs about English life. Nor were The Beatles the only group mining this vein. Songs by The Who, The Small Faces and especially The Kinks, all displayed a particularly English feel, be it the national obsession with eccentricity or lyrical phrasing that was unmistakably English or even London cockney slang.

'Arnold Layne' not only put Floyd into the Top 20 at their first attempt, but immediately established them as a 'name band'. With instant stardom came all the accompanying pressures. The beginning of Syd's breakdown was only weeks away but for a short while at least, life was glorious. Syd achieved one of his greatest ambitions on April 6 when Pink Floyd played for the first time on *Top Of The Pops*, then and now Britain's major television chart show. It was a great moment, but the band's workload – often playing to terminally unhip audiences – was mounting, along with the pressure to provide more hits.

The same night they appeared on *Top Of The Pops*, Floyd sped down the motorway for a gig at Salisbury. The following day they hired a plane to take them to a 'freak-out' in Belfast, Northern Ireland, where they were overwhelmed by the reception. The next week saw them appearing in Bishop's Stortford, Bath, Newcastle and Brighton. They had problems with their equipment and trouble getting public address systems to work properly because they played so loud. It was difficult because audiences who came to hear simple pop songs like 'Arnold Layne' encountered what *Melody Maker* called "a thundering, incomprehensible, screaming, sonic torture that five American doctors agree could permanently damage the senses . . ."

That month, Floyd were recorded for Granada Television in Manchester. The producer of the show asked them to appear on the same stage as The Move, so getting two bands for the price of one. Floyd wouldn't comply leaving the flustered producer remonstrating: 'I made The Beatles and I made The Stones.'

"It was a difficult situation," recalls Pip Carter who was struggling to maintain the Floyd's light show night after night. "I started to set up our lights and the whole lighting crew walked out because I was using a naked flame. I would light up this little gas burner and heat up the slides to make them jump.

"The Floyd meanwhile were threatening to walk out if they didn't get their way. Eventually everyone was placated and they went on and mimed to 'Arnold Layne' without The Move backing them."

One of the worst experiences happened at Feathers Club, Ealing, on April 24. Someone threw a penny (then the size of a 10 pence piece and every bit as heavy) from the largely hostile audience. It hit Roger Waters in the middle of his forehead, causing a huge cut. Waters, squaring up to the audience like the rugby three-quarter he once was, stood at the front of the stage bleeding heavily. He glowered into the audience, trying to see if he could catch the culprit throwing another coin, and prepared to leap into the audience to administer retribution.

Waters: "Happily there was one freak who liked us, so the audience spent the whole evening beating the shit out of him and left us alone."

On April 29, the Floyd headlined the 24-hour *Technicolour Dream* event at Alexandra Palace, a fund raiser for the still financially-troubled *International Times*. Forty-one groups offered to play and the Floyd took the stage in front of 10,000 people just as the pink glow of dawn tinted the huge east windows.

IT founder and Pink Floyd biographer Miles recalls: "Syd's eyes blazed as his notes soared up into the strengthening light and the dawn reflected in his mirror Telecaster guitar.

"I just couldn't believe it – outside, the straights of Wood Green were watching their tellies and inside this time-machine were thousands of stoned, tripping, mad, friendly, festive hippies. Talk about two different worlds!

"The thing that impressed me most was the lack of any sort of physical or mental barrier between performers and audience; when a band finished its set, the members got off stage and wandered into the crowd to sit on the floor."

Jenner: "It was a perfect setting. Everyone was waiting for the Floyd and everyone was on acid. That event was the peak of acid use in England . . . everyone was on it . . . the bands, the organisers, the audience . . . and I certainly was."

Floyd followed one triumph with another. On May 12 they gave the *Games For May* concert at the Queen Elizabeth Hall on London's South Bank – part of the arts complex building for the *Festival Of Britain* which was normally reserved for classical recitals. The concert was a milestone and paved the way for rock concerts of the seventies and eighties. Floyd played a lengthy set with no proper support act; in those days even headline acts never played more than 30 minutes.

A press release from The Christopher Hunt Agency read: "The Floyd intend this concert to be a musical and visual exploration – not only for themselves, but for the audience too. New material has been written and will be given for the first time, including some specially prepared four-way stereo tapes. Visually, the lights men of the group have prepared an entirely new, bigger-than-ever-before show.

"Sadly we are not allowed to throw lighting effects as planned onto the external surfaces of the hall, nor even the foyer, but inside should be enough!"

The huge speakers erected at the rear of the hall gave notice that the Floyd intended to utilise their much-vaunted Azimuth Co-ordinator for the first time. This would enable them to throw sound all round the hall, and in time the group would develop a full quadrophonic sound system. Audiences at Floyd concerts everywhere would henceforth crane their necks to see what they were missing behind them.

The group actually lost money on the *Games For May* concert, as they had to take a week off from other commitments to rehearse their show. An advert in *Melody Maker* six days beforehand announced: "Space-age relaxation for the climax of spring, electronic composition, colour and image projections, girls and the Pink Floyd."

Andrew King: "The *Games For May* concert was in two parts. There was a Floyd set in the second half and a number of individual efforts such as tape recordings in the first half."

Syd wrote a song called 'Games For May' especially for the event. A Floyd roadie put on an admiral's costume and threw daffodils into the audience, while a huge bubble machine filled the hall with spheres that reflected the lights and 35mm projections. Everyone went berserk. Everyone, that is, except the management of the hall, who were livid at the damage caused by trampled flowers and bursting bubbles which left circular soap stains on their plush seats. The event was talked about for weeks afterwards. Even that bastion of British conservative thinking, *The Financial Times*, was impressed and gave the show a favourable review. They reported: "The audience which filled the hall was beautiful, if strangely subdued, and to enjoy them was alone worth the price of a ticket. When you add in the irrepressible Pink Floyd and a free authentic daffodil to take home, your cup of experience overflows."

Syd's 'Games For May' composition, shortened but much the same in content, was developed as the next Floyd single under the new title 'See Emily Play'. Emily was a girl Syd claimed to have seen walking and dancing naked through some woods one morning when he had slept under the stars "after a gig up north."

Whether this romantic tale is true is debatable. Syd's unpredictable behaviour was becoming more evident by the day. By mid–1967 his LSD consumption was awesome. The heaven and hell visions it created formed the inspiration for much of his playing and writing but the drug was also the catalyst in his self-destruction. An unpleasant surprise was waiting for Dave Gilmour when he called in at The Chelsea Studios during the recording of 'See Emily Play'.

"Syd didn't seem to recognise me and just stared back," he says. "I got to know that look pretty well and I'll go on record as saying that that was when he changed. It was a shock. He was a different person. I assumed he'd had too much of the old substances, which is what everyone else thought."

Because Barrett's use of drugs was so apparent it was an easy mistake to assume the others followed a similar lifestyle. All four members of Pink Floyd smoked pot but the disciplined Waters had tried to ban it from recording sessions and had been known to snatch a joint from Syd's hand when in the studio. Mason, Wright and Waters may have dabbled with LSD but they were always more into booze than drugs.

Barrett was an enthusiastic advocate of LSD as early as 1965 and there is a persistent rumour that he once lived above the flat of a man believed to be the first LSD importer in Britain. A close friend of Syd's from Cambridge was the first man in Britain to be convicted of possessing the drug shortly after it was made illegal.

Considering Barrett's heavy drug usage, it is understandable that his already eccentric behaviour became progressively stranger. On one occasion he was driving his Mini along the King's Road in Chelsea when his attention was drawn to an item of clothing in a shop on the opposite side of the street. Syd stopped the car at some traffic lights, jumped out, and loped across the busy road, leaving the car engine running, an open-mouthed friend in the passenger seat, and a line of fuming motorists behind him.

Pete Townshend was an admirer of Syd's wild chord playing but realised that by the time he got to know the Floyd, Barrett was "pretty fucked up."

"There is no question that Syd had something special, but if Roger Waters hadn't been there I don't think Syd would have been able to find his way to the stage to be quite honest," says Townshend. "He seemed to spend most of the time setting up echoes in the machines he used. You would hear a guitar playing then suddenly you realised he'd gone off stage, was fiddling with an amp or sitting in a chair. You didn't quite know where the sound was coming from. But if Syd was innovative at anything, it was at getting completely and totally out of it. He was the first person I had seen who was totally 'gone' on stage. I'd never have done that and neither would anyone I knew because there was still a tremendous amount of reverence towards the audience.

"Syd was only able to get away with it because he could count on most of the audience being out of their brains as well. Funnily enough, the person who did scare the shit out of me was Roger Waters. He had such a fearsome countenance both on and off stage. Syd was pitiful and tragic in comparison."

Keith West, lead singer with Tomorrow, the British group best remembered for their 1967 song 'My White Bicycle', was another who witnessed Syd's strange behaviour. The first of many experiences was when the Floyd's leader was frying an egg over a small camping stove on the stage at UFO during a performance.

"Syd was very vague conversationally and you couldn't really communicate with him. Later that year when we were sharing a hotel in Rotterdam with the Floyd, the other members of the band were trying to communicate by passing notes to him."

Syd's sister Rosemary, who had been so excited by the success of the first single, realised that something was going dreadfully wrong. "The next time I saw him he'd changed so much that I couldn't reach him. The brother I knew had disappeared. After that meeting I just couldn't enjoy the music any more."

In October 1988, the writer Jonathon Meades told *The News Of The World:* "In 1967 Syd stayed with some mates in a mansion block right opposite South Kensington tube station. I went to visit them one night and suddenly there was this terrible noise. It sounded like water pipes rattling and shaking. 'God,' I said, 'What on earth is that?' They all started giggling and said: 'Oh, that's just Syd on a bad trip again. We always lock him in the linen cupboard'."

The most vivid description of Syd's disintegration came from Joe Boyd. "The Floyd hadn't played at UFO for two months or something and they came back for their first gig after really making it. I remember it was really crowded. They came past me, just inside the door. It was very crushed so it was like faces two inches from your nose. I greeted them all as they came through. The last one was Syd and the great thing with Syd was that he had a twinkle in his eye. I mean he was a real eye-twinkler. He had this impish look about him, this mischievous glint. He came by, and I said: 'Hi Syd.' He just kind of looked at me. I looked right in his eye and there was no twinkle, no glint. It was like somebody had pulled the blinds – you know, nobody home. It was a real shock. Very, very sad."

Chapter Five

The Piper At The Gates Of Dawn

A fter signing Pink Floyd EMI lost no time in deciding to drop Joe Boyd as their producer and bring in their house producer, Norman Smith. Smith had never wanted 'Arnold Layne'to go out in its Boyd-produced form and had the support of Waters and Wright. Syd, however, had flatly refused to cut another version and got his own way. When it came to 'See Emily Play' it was Syd who opposed the single release for reasons he did not care to explain. Smith could only speculate that: "He had this thing about commercialism."

Ironically, when the group went into Abbey Road Studios with Smith, they spent plenty of EMI's money desperately trying to recapture the sound Boyd had created so effortlessly. They eventually had to trudge back to Sound Techniques after scrubbing the work they had already done.

Much comment has been made on the soaring guitar solo that was the centrepiece of 'Emily' – one of Barrett's most widely remembered works. Smith: "We used frequency control to speed up Syd's guitar playing. It was things like that that really intrigued me."

'Emily' was completed on May 23 and, despite Barrett's protests, released on June 16. It climbed to number six in the charts the following month. Critics who felt 'Arnold Layne' was not psychedelic enough, agreed that the follow-up more than compensated.

Procol Harum's Gary Brooker, guesting on *Melody Maker's* 'Blind Date' spot, recognised the Floyd sound almost immediately. "I can tell by that horrible organ," he wrote. "They are the only people doing this kind of scene and they have a very distinctive sound. It's much better than 'Arnold Layne' – much better. If 'Arnold Layne' was a hit then this should be more of a hit.''

NME reviewer Derek Johnson spotlighted the new Floyd disc under the banner headline: 'Melody survives the Pink Floyd happening.' He wrote: "On Pink Floyd's last disc, the psychedelia in which they specialise didn't really come through but, golly, they've made up for it on this new one. It's crammed with weird oscillations, reverberations, electronic vibrations and fuzzy rumblings. Surprisingly, somewhere amid the happening there's also a pleasant mid-tempo tune that's appealingly harmonised. Should register!"

Commenting on the flip side 'Scarecrow' – another Barrett composition (and the subject of a surreal Floyd promo film) – Johnson added: "Interesting, fascinating harmonies, clip-clop rhythm, old world flute, nice acoustic guitar."

In a notable U-turn Radio London, uncomfortably aware that it was missing out on the Flower Power scene, made 'Emily' number one on their 'Big L' chart in the week of its release. The chart bore no relation to sales – being compiled on the whim of the programme director – but it did the record no harm.

Floyd promoted 'Emily' three times on *Top Of The Pops*. The first week Syd appeared in his latest satin and velvet acquisition from the trendy Kings Road boutique Granny Takes A Trip. A week later, he was unshaven and the immaculate clothes were dirty and creased. The third week he arrived in his Kings Road finest, only to change backstage into the scruffiest rags he had been able to dig out.

Waters: "He didn't want to know. He got down there in an incredible state and said he wasn't going to do it. We finally discovered the reason was that John Lennon didn't have to do it so he didn't . . ."

Smith: "Syd had been in the make-up department and came out looking terrific. He walked up to the mirror, took one look and messed his hair all up muttering, 'It's rubbish . . . rubbish!'"

The world at large and Syd's growing number of fans had no idea anything was wrong. To them it was lovable old Syd playing the star again. Around this period Syd was involved in an incident which seemed little more than a temperamental fit, but which later took on much greater significance. The band were booked to appear on the famous *Saturday Club* radio programme in London but a series of production difficulties kept them waiting to perform their set for most of the day. Finally the troubles were sorted out and Floyd were about to perform when Syd suddenly walked out of the studio saying: "I'm never doing this again." Waters ran outside only to see him disappearing into the distance. The session was abandoned.

Nevertheless Syd's growing reputation as a songwriter and innovative guitarist had already established him as the star of the group. With 'Emily' riding high in the charts, he was invited to fill the 'Blind Date' spot. Coincidently, it shared a page that week with a feature on Jimi Hendrix, Syd's favourite musician at that time.

The records *Melody Maker* thrust upon Syd ranged from the largely unknown David Bowie's whimsical 'Love You Till Tuesday' to Vince Hill's MOR ballad 'When The World Is Ready'. Syd enjoyed Alex Harvey's 'The Sunday Song' ("Nice sounds. Yeah. Wow.") but found Barry Fantoni's 'Nothing Today' very negative. He also considered Jim Reeves' 'Trying To Forget' very way-out.

"I don't know who it was. Well, let me think – who's dead? It must be Jim Reeves. I don't think it will be a hit. It doesn't matter if an artist is dead or alive about records being released. But if you're trendy this doesn't quite fit the bill."

Syd was also invited to pass comment on 'One By One' by The Blue Magoos: "You're going to tell me it's The Byrds. I really dig The Byrds, Mothers Of Invention and The Fugs. We have drawn quite a bit from those groups."

Although the Floyd considered themselves above the triviality of the pop scene, they relented on one occasion and agreed to appear in the *NME* 'Lifelines' series which quizzed popular artists about everything from their favourite colour and food to the pets they kept.

Rick Wright revealed that his first public appearance was "in the bath" and that drunks, crowded pubs, violence and difficult situations (including music paper questionnaires) constituted his miscellaneous dislikes. Nick Mason listed his biggest career influences as "fear and rum" and disclosed his modest ambition to rule the world. Waters sarcastically listed his parents' names as "mum and dad" and attributed his musical education to "12 years tuition on the spoons."

Syd, for his part, told *NME* readers that his favourite drink was Campari and soda and that he had no hobbies but did own a cat named Rover.

Floyd's growing status was further illustrated by some unlikely press reporting towards the end of July. The band, it seemed, were to play at an official Youth Culture festival of music at the 1968 Olympic Games in Mexico City.

In fact the group were planning a lengthy concert tour to promote their forthcoming début album and a recent gig at The Roundhouse had been filmed for a *Man Alive* TV special on the venue. The world was at their feet.

With 'Emily' still at number five in the *Melody Maker* charts, Floyd travelled 'north of the border' for the first time, albeit for only two shows. They included both hits for their Scottish fans but on their return to UFO the band played their usual two sets and ignored both singles. They did include 'Pow R Toc H' and a new number called 'Reaction In G' – a protest against being called to perform 'Emily'.

While Floyd thought the success of their singles was a double-edged sword, EMI had no such doubts. All apprehensions about drug connections forgotten, the company arranged at once for Norman Smith to produce the album.

Smith had joined EMI in 1959 as a recording assistant at Abbey Road, working with Beatles' producer George Martin. When Martin headed off to form his own company in 1965, Smith was left behind as producer with EMI's Parlophone label and continued to engineer on Beatles' sessions.

Smith first saw Pink Floyd perform at UFO in the company of their publisher Bryan Morrison. "I didn't have a clue what Syd's songs were about and I suspect the other band members didn't either," he says. "But the amount of press coverage they were receiving helped sway me to decide EMI should have them."

Andrew King was with Floyd every day during the recording of the album. "It was all done pretty quickly – about one song a day. Considering it was a first album, it was fairly experimental. There were some unusual things with double tracking and overdubbing of whole performances over each other – as on 'Interstellar Overdrive'. The stereo split which Norman did was a bit ham-fisted, but it worked."

Syd (nee Roger), aged 18 months. *(Barrett Family Collection)*

Syd, aged 4, with his sister Rosemary, aged 2. *(Barrett Family Collection)*

Syd, aged 6, at London Zoo *(Barrett Family Collection)*

Syd, aged 13, at Boy Scout Camp *(Barrett Family Collection)*

Syd with Frisky, the family cat, in the garden at Hills Road, Cambridge. *(Barrett Family Collection)*

Left: Roger Waters, aged 16, fly-half for the Cambridge High School Rugby XV. *(Photographer unknown* Right: A youthful Dave Gilmour swims the River Cam. *(Photographer unknown)*

Joker's Wild, featuring Dave Gilmour on guitar, playing at a private party in Cambridge in the early '60s. Left to right: Gilmour, John Gordon, Clive Welham, unknown. *(Phtographer unknown)*

Syd and Libby Gausden on holiday at Butlins, June 1962. *(Photographer unknown)*

Pink Floyd, 1964. Left to right: Syd Barrett, Bob Klose, Chris Dennis, Roger Waters.
(Photographer unknown)

Returning to Cambridge, Syd performs with Those Without, January 2, 1965. Left to right: Syd, 'Smudge', Stephen Pyle, unknown. *(Photographer unknown)*

Pink Floyd, 1965, in the garden of their Highgate flat. Left to right: Roger Waters, Nick Mason, Syd, Bob Klose, Rick Wright. *(Photographer unknown)*

Pink Floyd perform at the Middle Earth Club in London's Covent Garden, 1966.
(Pictorial Press)

Syd, rehearsing with Roger Waters, in 1966. *(Irene Winsby)*

Pink Floyd jump for joy outside EMI's Manchester Square offices after signing their first record contract in 1967... *(Pictorial Press)*

...And pose for the cameras again with instruments but no leads later the same day. *(Photographer unknown)*

Stereo production ideas weren't the only thing to advance in
the intervening years . . . "There was a knob on the mixing desk
which had 'pop' on one side and 'classical' on the other. I always
wondered what it did," recalls King.

Floyd's co-manager invariably arrived at the studio around
lunchtime and was always under the impression that the
sessions were progressing well. Smith remembers things very
differently. He had already run into serious problems with Syd.
"When I look back at that album, I wonder how we managed to
get anything together. Working with Syd was sheer hell and
there are no pleasant memories. I don't think I left a single Floyd
session without a splitting headache. Syd never seemed to have
any enthusiasm for anything. He would be singing a song and
I'd call him into the control room to give a few instructions. Then
he'd go back out and not even sing the first part the same, let
alone the bit I'd been talking about. Sometimes he even changed
the words – he just had no discipline.

"Trying to talk to him was like trying to talk to a brick wall
because his face was so expressionless. His lyrics were simple
and child-like and he was like a child in many ways – up one
minute and down the next. I often wondered what the hell he
was doing in the music business. The other guys seemed to
think he had something, though."

Like many to follow, Smith discovered there was only one
way to record Syd Barrett – his way!

"Syd would play his songs to the others and eventually get
something down on tape. Then we would all try and knock it
into shape. Once we had something down on the master tape,
that was it as far as Syd was concerned. He genuinely wanted to
put it out in its raw, unfinished state."

Smith was equally unimpressed with the rest of Pink Floyd.
"Waters wasn't a great bass player but learnt fast enough. I
always thought Wright was quietly arrogant and believed he
was a better organist than he actually was. Mason was just along
for the ride, waiting for the money to roll in so he could go off
with his beloved motor cars."

While Floyd were recording in studios two and three, The
Beatles were next door finishing 'Sgt. Pepper's Lonely Hearts
Club Band'. "They were in awe of The Beatles," says Smith.
"Syd seemed to get more of a kick out of meeting them than he
got out of actually being in the Floyd."

King: "I don't know how often the Floyd popped next door, but I went in once when The Beatles were mixing 'Lovely Rita'. The bad vibes in that studio were, if anything, worse than in the Floyd sessions."

Smith: "Paul McCartney happened to be working alone in studio two on my first evening session with the Floyd in number three. I was nervous as hell but Paul gave me a big boost by telling the Floyd they had the best producer in the business."

McCartney later told the press that Floyd's album was "a knockout."

While Norman Smith bore the brunt of Syd's eccentric behaviour, Peter Jenner stood back in awe of him. "Syd had a unique way of mixing," says Jenner. "He would throw the levers on the board up and down, apparently at random, making pretty patterns with his hands. He was very demanding. You see, he was a painter and would not do anything unless he was doing it in an artistic way. He was 100 per cent creative and very hard on himself."

Barrett's influences ranged far and wide. Although UFO fans always associated him with his far-out space songs, most of his writing was more down to earth. There were only two real space songs, 'Astronomy Domine' and 'Interstellar Overdrive', and the latter had been written almost by accident.

Jenner: "I was once trying to tell Syd about this Arthur Lee song I couldn't remember the title of ('My Little Red Book'), so I just hummed the main riff. Syd picked up his guitar and followed what I was humming. The pattern he worked out went on to become the main riff for 'Interstellar Overdrive'."

Although the nine-minute-plus classic is credited to all four band members, Syd's theme emphasises his dominant role at that stage. The other sections of the album recording were basically condensed passages of his undisciplined UFO guitar experimentation with Mason's drums providing melody as well as rhythm, Wright hanging ethereal chords where appropriate and Waters following Syd's main riff as best he could. Contrary to popular belief it was not pinched from the theme to television's *Steptoe And Son*.

Waters told *Q* magazine in 1987: "Syd as a writer was a one-off. I could never aspire to his crazed insights and perceptions. In fact, for a long time I wouldn't have dreamed of claiming any insights whatsoever. But I'd always credit Syd with the connection he made to his personal subconscious and to the collective group subconscious. It's taken me 15 years to get anywhere near there. But what enabled Syd to see things the way he did? It's like why is an artist an artist? Artists simply do feel and see things in a different way to other people. In a way it's a blessing, but it can also be a terrible curse. There's a great deal of satisfaction to be earned from it, but often it's also a terrible burden."

The song 'Chapter 24' came from the *I Ching*, the Chinese Book of Changes, a 5,000 year-old Taoist book of oracles used as a guide in life-problems and for divination of the future. Along with tarot cards, it became a popular diversion among the trendy young of the late sixties. Any problem was first framed as a question. Then, by throwing six coins representing six lines of yes or no, 64 combinations (answers) could be consulted. The answers, set out as chapters in the *I Ching*, were cryptic and could be interpreted several ways. Syd's consultation referred him to Chapter 24 – *Fu*, or Return/The Turning Point. Richard Wilhelm, in his translation of the classic, first published in 1951 and the most likely source for Barrett's lyrics, gave the judgement as follows:

'Return. Success.
Going out and coming in without error.
Friends come without blame.
To and fro goes the way.
On the seventh day comes return.
It furthers one to have somewhere to go.'

Wilhelm went on to translate: "All movements are accomplished in six stages, and the seventh brings return" – the opening lines to Barrett's song, almost to the word. And, later: "Therefore seven is the number of the young light, and it arises when six, the number of the great darkness, is increased by one." (Routledge and Kegan Paul, Third Edition, 1968.) The attraction for the increasingly pressurised Barrett was clear, for Chapter 24, *Fu*, described the discarding of the old and the introduction of the new, resulting in harmony.

Matthew Scurlow: "In those days it was very élitist stuff, along with Jung. It was on the periphery of being trendy but, as happened so often, Syd discovered it before anyone else and was the first of our generation to consult the oracle as such."

Barrett's Cambridge girlfriend, Jenny, turns up in the menac-ing 'Lucifer Sam' which contains the line: 'Jennifer gentle, you're a witch . . .' – possibly written during one of the couple's many splits.

The dopey, Hobbit-like lyrics of 'The Gnome' came off the top of Syd's head during an earlier richly-creative period. Pip Carter claimed to have once seen Syd put music to 60 pieces of poetry in one session, one of which, 'Golden Hair', appeared on his first solo album.

'The Piper At The Gates Of Dawn' was released on August 5, 1967 to almost universal acclaim. Syd had taken the title from a chapter heading in his favourite children's book, *The Wind In The Willows* by Kenneth Grahame – a novel which effectively captures the tranquil atmosphere of Grantchester Meadows where many of Barrett's earliest songs took shape on the acoustic guitar.

Syd also designed the psychedelic artwork on the back of the sleeve, reminiscent of the UFO bubble slide show.

His own recollections of the album seemed quite satisfied. Talking to Giovanni Dadomo in 1970, he said: "It was difficult in some ways getting used to the studio and everything, but it was fun. We freaked out a lot."

Dadomo: "How important are the lyrics?"

Barrett: "Very important. I think it's good if a song has more than one meaning. Maybe that song can reach far more people, that's nice. On the other hand, I like songs that are simple. I like 'Arnold Layne' because to me that's a very clear song."

During the chat Barrett revealed that 'Lucifer Sam' was another song influenced by the *I Ching*. "It did not mean much to me at the time, but then, three to four months later, it came to mean a lot."

Asked if he was ever a science fiction fan, Syd replied: "Not really, except *Journey Into Space* and *Quatermass*, which was when I was about 15. That could be where it comes from."

A disappointing feature of the album to many Floyd followers was the conservative nature of the sleeve – a rather unimagina-tive picture of the four members in a kaleidoscopic effect. Syd, sitting there in his Kings Road finery, manages to muster sufficient poise, but Waters, Wright and Mason have the look of men who, having boarded a number 10 bus to Clapham, discover they've mistakenly hitched a ride on an intergalactic juggernaut.

Some of the UFO purists felt the record failed to capture the excitement of the group's experimental stage sound. Pete Townshend was one of its strongest critics: "I thought it was fucking awful and had so little to do with what they did live. It was like bubblegum – Mickey Mouse music – and I thought the guy who produced it was a tosser."

Elsewhere, rave reviews poured in. The ousted Joe Boyd might have been expected to be amongst the first critics. Instead he enthused: "I think 'The Piper At The Gates Of Dawn' is a great album and really well produced . . . I think 'Bike' for instance is one of the greatest tracks of all time."

Allen Evans of the *NME* gave 'Piper' four stars in his September 9 review, noting Barrett's major contribution: "The rasping guitar is very much to the fore and the vocals are largely distorted. Shouts and raving laughs come in suddenly and there is some raving organ from Rick Wright in Muddy Waters' 'Take Up Thy Stethoscope And Walk'. One very long track, 'Interstellar Overdrive', takes up most of side two with its weird, extra-loud overtones. Nick Mason's drum effects on 'Scarecrow' are good too."

Roger Waters' reaction to seeing his sole songwriting contribution attributed to Muddy Waters can easily be imagined.

Ten years later in a lengthy article on Barrett in the American *Trouser Press* magazine, Kris DiLorenzo stressed the importance of Floyd's début album: "Barrett's music was as experimental as you could get without crossing over entirely into freeform jazz. There simply were no other bands extending the boundaries of rock beyond the basic sex and love themes.

"His trademark and Achilles heel was sudden surprise. Trance-like riffs would slide abruptly into intense, slightly offbeat strumming ('Astronomy Domine'), choppy urgency gives way to powerful, frightening peaks ('Interstellar Overdrive'), harmless lyrics skitter over a fierce undertow of evil-sounding feedback and menacing wah-wah ('Lucifer Sam').

"His work with Pink Floyd still ranks as some of the most expressive sensational playing recorded by a rock guitarist. Yet Syd borrowed no familiar licks, as the young Eric Clapton, Jeff Beck and Jimmy Page were wont to.

"Barrett's songwriting genius was original and extremist as well. His singing was highly stylised – obscure, chanting vocals, high-tension verses and explosive choruses, alternating with dead-pan story-telling and hypnotic drawls. He utilised fairy-tale technique, surrealistic juxtaposition of psychedelic detail and plain fact, childhood experience and adult confusion.

"Indisputably, Barrett was an innovator. Whether he was entirely conscious or in control of his art is impossible to determine."

'The Piper At The Gates Of Dawn' is now regarded as one of the best albums ever made. The 20th anniversary edition of *Rolling Stone* in 1987 placed it 79th on the all-time list, asserting that "Pink Floyd's début blast of psycho-acid fury was to England's first flowering of psychedelia what The Jefferson Airplane's 'Surrealistic Pillow' was to San Francisco's Summer Of Love."

Rolling Stone added: "'The Piper At The Gates Of Dawn' . . . wrapped the various mutant pop strains coursing through the British paisley underground – Whoish pop-art violence, neo-jazz improvisation, LSD-spiked Tolkienesque whimsy – into a dazzling mural of otherworldly rock 'n' roll madness. The madness was very real as well: the founder and main songwriter, Syd Barrett, was already on his way to a drug-fuelled psychological collapse when the LP was released . . .

"Yet it is the combination of the original Floyd's vigorous future-rock pursuits and Barrett's teetering on the precipice of reality that makes 'Piper' such a riveting experience. (The rest of the Floyd) frame Barrett's acid-refracted observations of fairy-tale folk . . . with haunting, often disorientating chamber-pop arrangements." *Rolling Stone*, August 27, 1987.

Syd was never to recapture the magic of that first album. By August 1967, amid the furore of its release, there were persistent rumours that all was not well in the Floyd camp. There was even talk that Syd had left the group after the cancellation of a promotional trip to Germany and a one-nighter in Torquay.

Andrew King put on a brave face and assured the *NME* that while Syd had not left the group, he was tired and had been advised to rest for two weeks. When the news conscious *Melody Maker* got wind of the story on August 19, it produced a special edition with the front page headline proclaiming in bold print: 'PINK FLOYD FLAKE OUT'.

Syd's problem was now clearly more serious than first thought. He was suffering from nervous exhaustion which forced the group to cancel all work until the end of the month – losing them £4000. All four were packed off to Spain for some rest.

As a result, Floyd were unable to appear at the prestigious *Windsor National Jazz And Blues Festival*, where disenchanted fans booed ex-Manfred Mann singer Paul Jones when he announced the band were not coming.

Chapter Six

Blown On The Steel Breeze

Hoping to put all the recent difficulties behind them, Andrew King lined up a short series of gigs to introduce Pink Floyd to the potentially vast American audience. They left for the States on October 24 but were to return just one week later after a catalogue of disasters.

The eternally optimistic King had booked three nights at Bill Graham's Fillmore West in San Francisco on October 26, 27 and 28. A number of television appearances were also planned. King had flown out three days earlier only to find to his horror that he could not get the band into the country.

"They were late because of work permit problems and ended up being the first band not to turn up at Fillmore West. I had three days of promoter Bill Graham going berserk. Finally we had to telephone the Vice-President at about five in the morning to get everything fixed. That was a pretty poor start and when we finally arrived we found our light show was a joke.

"Our lights looked pathetic in San Francisco. The whole show was laughable by today's standards of high technology. We thought we were doing it better than them because our effects were more clever and more interesting. Maybe they were – our coloured strobes were quite extraordinary – but they tended to blow up every 10 seconds so they were rarely working.

"In America they had the big powerful stuff but we just did not have that sort of gear. The biggest lamp we had was a single kilowatt bulb but a typical West Coast show had 20 10-kilowatt bulbs. The only things that really worked were the more powerful slide projections.

"The old Fillmore looked like a big church hall and held about 2000 people, then there was the larger Winterland. The first night in the smaller place made quite an impression but the next night in the Winterland we were totally blown away."

Third on the bill to Janis Joplin's Big Brother And The Holding Company and Richie Havens, Floyd were expecting "something way-out." Instead they were dismayed to find they were preceding blues-rock acts. Not surprisingly, they went down like a lead balloon.

King: "It was lack of experience really. Basically, we should not have gone out when we did. I had no way of realising how completely out to lunch the record company was. It was a subsidiary of Capitol. When we went for a meeting with the managing director he burst into tears and asked us what he was going to do."

'Out to lunch' also perfectly described Syd's state on the ill-advised venture. The problems came to a head on the US pop TV show *Dick Clark's American Bandstand* which had a mainly teenage audience. Floyd were scheduled to mime 'See Emily Play' for which the television technicians had devised a primitive video effect simulating swirling clouds.

King: "It was ghastly. Syd wasn't into moving his lips that day so we had to pretend Roger sang while Syd just stood there."

On *The Pat Boone Show*, the genial host fired a barrage of inane questions at Syd whose only reply was a totally disinterested stare.

Barrett's patience finally snapped during the recording of a third television show. His walkout prompted the cancellation of Floyd's appearance.

King can laugh about it now: "This American TV producer, who looked like Kojak with his bald head and cool shades, said: 'Wha'd'ya mean the lead guitarist has gone?' There was no way he could (mimicking American accent) 'relate to this concept' on his show!"

Further gigs had been pencilled in for Chicago and New York, but at this stage King, whose nerves – like everyone else's – had been reduced to ribbons, decided to cut his losses. The East Coast never saw Syd's Pink Floyd.

During their stay in Los Angeles, Floyd met up with the original Alice Cooper band, confirmed Barrett fans since hearing 'Piper At The Gates Of Dawn'. Cooper had hired a house in the Venice area while they appeared as house band at The Cheetah

Club, and he invited Pink Floyd to dinner. Guitarist Glen Buxton – not the most stable fellow himself – was knocked out by their enigmatic leader, and described his brief acquaintance with Syd in an interview with the New York-based *Trouser Press* magazine in 1978.

"I don't remember him ever saying two words. It wasn't because he was a snob. He was a very strange person. He never talked but we'd be sitting at dinner and all of a sudden I'd pick up the sugar and pass it to him. It was like I heard him say: 'Pass the sugar.' It was like telepathy – it really was. You'd find yourself in the middle of something and think: 'Well damn! I didn't hear anyone say anything.' That was the first time in my life I'd ever met anyone who could actually do that freely. And this guy did it all the time – he was definitely from Mars."

The account suggests that if anyone was spaced out it was Buxton, and such stories did much to exaggerate and glamorise Syd's precarious state. As the pressure on the Floyd increased, so too did the demand on Barrett as 'chief egg-layer'. Even before the end of the American tour he was being pushed to come up with a third hit single. His continued ferocious drug intake only exacerbated the problem and the writer's response was to grow steadily more insular and erratic.

When things became too much, Syd would literally drop everything and go walkabout. Other times his chronic absent-mindedness resulted in his famous Fender Telecaster being left behind at the previous venue, resulting in a frantic and expensive trip to recover the precious instrument. The Floyd tried dealing with Syd's problems but tempers were flaring and patience growing thin. On the flight home to England, Waters and Mason at least had made up their minds – something was going to have to change.

There was no respite back in Blighty. They were hustled into Abbey Road to record 'Paintbox' on November 2. They soon realised that this was not to be a hit single and besides, Syd told Norman Smith he wanted a Salvation Army band for a possible new single called 'Jugband Blues'. The producer was somewhat taken aback but sufficiently familiar with Syd's hare-brained notions to do as instructed or face a walkout.

"I went to the trouble of booking a band but of course Syd was late turning up as usual. I told the band they were going to meet

Syd Barrett and were in for a *very* odd session – even I did not know what was going to happen. Syd eventually arrived and I introduced him to the players. He had no plan of what he wanted at all and just said: 'Let them play what they like.' The session lasted six hours and was a hell of a struggle. Syd got bored after half-an-hour and announced he was going home. I was glad because he was more of a hindrance than a help. When I played the finished song to him he simply said: 'Yeah, that's OK'."

The crazy 'Jugband Blues' sessions at the De Lane Lea Studios did at least produce a couple of, as yet unreleased, Barrett tracks, 'Scream Thy Last Scream' and 'Vegetable Man' which collectors now drool over. The two songs have periodically surfaced on illegal bootleg collections over the years. In a 1974 *NME* article on Barrett, Nick Kent described the first as "a masterful splurge of blood-curdling, pre-Beefheartian lunacy." Pete Jenner maintains that Syd wrote 'Vegetable Man' in a matter of minutes by simply describing what he was wearing at the time and throwing in a chorus that went: 'Vegetable man, where are you?' – a phrase that accurately summed up his mental condition.

Jenner: "Syd knew what was happening to him. 'Jugband Blues' is the ultimate self-diagnosis on a state of schizophrenia . . ."

'Jugband Blues' (excerpt).

'It's awfully considerate of you to think of me here,
And I'm most obliged to you for making it clear
. . . that I'm not here,
And I'm wondering who could be writing this song . . .'

Syd had always had a sardonic sense of humour and there were suggestions that the last line was a dig at the rest of the group on how they might manage without him.

Jenner: "I think we tended to underrate the extent of his problem. One thing I regret now is that I made demands on Syd. He'd written 'See Emily Play' and suddenly everything had to be seen in commercial terms. I think we pressurised him into a state of paranoia about having to come up with another hit single."

A third single was eventually dragged out of the reluctant star. 'Apples And Oranges' was released on November 18 with

Rick Wright's 'Paintbox' on the flipside. Syd apparently wrote the song about a girl he saw shopping around Richmond and described it as a happy song with "a touch of Christmas." The music press predicted a surefire hit but the adage 'third time lucky' did not hold true. The disc sank without trace giving Pink Floyd their first experience of failure.

The disappointment was compounded by a disastrous short tour of Holland when Syd's on-stage contribution effectively dried up completely. He had been playing less and less over the preceding months and by November would often spend an entire gig playing the same chord over and over again while staring blankly at the audience. On other nights he would freeze with his arm hanging limply over his Telecaster, or sit cross-legged at the front of the stage seemingly oblivious to the performance going on around him.

Storm Thorgeson: "I remember seeing the Floyd play one night and suddenly realising that Syd was playing a completely different tune to the rest of the band or such a different variation that the others were having trouble following it. Some people may say he played only one note because he was a genius but I don't buy that shit – if you're in a band, you're in a band. Syd was beginning to be a real drag – a megalomaniac, divorced from reality. He seemed to travel in his own mind and got more and more interested in the edges of his personality which separated him from the rest of the group."

The individual who took the brunt of Barrett's brainstorms was his long-time girlfriend Lynsey Korner, still living with him in a flat on Richmond Hill. Lynsey had always regarded Syd as "the sweetest, kindest, most together person imaginable" but shortly after the release of 'Emily', chronic schizophrenia set in and by Christmas even Lynsey admitted "Syd was beginning to act a little bonkers."

She soon paid for his worsening condition. One of LSD's more tangible side effects are sudden violent rages, but Pete Jenner was not to know that when Lynsey appeared on his doorstep one morning quite badly beaten up. He and the others couldn't accept that Syd was responsible and still failed to realise the full extent of his drug dependence.

A few weeks later Syd accompanied an old Cambridge friend, Nigel Lesmoire-Gordon, and a couple of other LSD freaks on a crazy weekend trip to Andrew King's Herefordshire cottage. Lesmoire-Gordon recalls Syd spending an entire night hanging on an overhead beam and rocking his heels back and forth on a lemonade bottle. He admits disarmingly: "By that stage it was difficult to tell who was mad and who wasn't."

Midway through November, Floyd took part in a nationwide tour of Britain knowing that even if their guitarist and singer turned up, he would produce little on stage. It was the last proper Harold Davidson one-nighter pop package and featured seven groups including Amen Corner, The Move, and The Jimi Hendrix Experience. The tour opened at London's Royal Albert Hall on November 14 and took in Bournemouth, Leeds, Liverpool, Nottingham, Portsmouth, Bristol, Cardiff, Manchester, Belfast, Chatham and Brighton up to December 2.

King: "Really we shouldn't have done that tour for Syd's sake but the shows were a lot of fun and it was good in a way because it got us lots of exposure."

Syd was impossible – often late, sometimes absent. When the tour bus arrived at its destination he would often stay in his seat or simply wander off minutes before he was due on stage. On these nights, Davy O'List of The Nice sometimes stood in for him.

Syd was into anarchic experiments which naturally alienated him from the rest of the band. Waters and the others had a growing feeling that he was trying to make them look stupid while noting the growing list of promoters who made it clear they would not be invited back. Barrett's last major gig was the *Christmas On Earth Revisited* show at Olympia on December 22. Hendrix, The Move and The Soft Machine were in the line-up but the proceedings were far from memorable at the spacious atmosphere-lacking venue. Syd's arms hung limply by his sides as Floyd struggled through their set without his active participation.

King: "Things were terrible on stage. No one really played anything except Roger Waters who kept playing the same bass pattern over and over while everyone else just stood there not knowing what to do."

Syd had finally brought his free-form ideas to a logical if unsatisfactory conclusion.

Nick Mason: "We staggered on thinking we couldn't manage without Syd. So we put up with what can only be described as a fucking maniac. We didn't choose to use those words, but I think he was."

Waters: "The thing got to the point where we had to say to Syd that he should leave because we respected him as a writer but his live performances were useless. He was working out so many things none of us understood. He would detune his guitar and strum the loose strings. We used to come off stage bleeding because we hit things in frustration."

Waters, Mason and Wright agreed that the logical replacement was Dave Gilmour who was back in London and living on the breadline after working for a year in France. Mason: "We were teaching Dave the numbers with the idea that we were going to be a five-piece. Then Syd came in with some new material. The song went 'Have You Got It Yet?' but he kept changing it so no one could learn it."

Waters: "It was a real act of mad genius. The interesting thing about it was that I didn't suss it out at all. I stood there for about an hour while he was singing: 'Have you got it yet?' and I'd sing: 'No, no.' Terrific!"

Floyd played five gigs as a five-piece – the first at Aston University, Birmingham – then reached the conclusion that it was pointless Barrett coming on just to ruin things.

The five-man Floyd posed stoically for a photo session that January. In one of the pictures, the gaunt hollow-eyed Barrett hovers behind Waters and Mason, almost totally obscured by their shoulders. The clear shot of Waters, Mason, Wright and Gilmour contrasts sharply with the out of focus Barrett. Whether by accident or design, the photographer failed to adjust his depth of field leaving the ghostly image of Syd in the background, a fitting comment on his current status in the group.

The point of no return came on March 2. Waters: "We had a big meeting at Ladbroke Road which came down to me and Syd sitting in a room talking. I'd worked out what I thought was the only way we could carry on together, which was for him to become a sort of Brian Wilson figure, write the songs and come to recording sessions. By the end of the afternoon I thought I'd convinced him that it was a good idea but it didn't mean much because he was likely to totally change his mind about anything in an hour. He went home and I went to see Peter and Andrew and said that this was the end – if this didn't work out then we were off. They didn't see things the same way that I saw it. We never saw them again except at meetings to dissolve the partnership. We had to sort out who owned what, but that was the end that day."

King: "Basically we sided with Syd. We thought Pink Floyd had no future without him. If you like we were Syd groupies – that is certainly what Roger Waters would say. He would say we thought the sun shone out of Syd's backside and had no faith in the rest of the band – a bit harsh, but largely true."

The split was not publicised until April 6 but Barrett's musical contribution was effectively over as early as January. He left about a quarter of the way through the recording of the second album 'Saucerful Of Secrets'. The record closed with Syd's 'Jugband Blues' which took on a new poignancy following his breakdown and subsequent departure. He also played on Rick Wright's 'Remember A Day' – a leftover from the 'Piper' sessions – and possibly on another Wright composition 'See Saw' as well as Waters' 'Set The Controls For The Heart Of The Sun'. Syd apparently waited in EMI's Abbey Road reception for a couple of days, guitar in hand, waiting to make another contribution. The call never came.

While Syd's psychedelic juggernaut was soaring to dizzy heights, his eventual replacement had been experiencing the other side of the rock 'n' roll tracks. Dave Gilmour, working with a reduced version of Jokers Wild in France, often wondered where his next meal was coming from. Along with guitarist Rick Wills and drummer Willie Wilson, Gilmour had set off on his European odyssey after the original members had split acrimoniously.

They initially tried their luck in Spain before making their way to France in late 1966. The following spring saw them in Paris where their van was broken into and all their microphones stolen. Gilmour was duly dispatched on a rescue mission to bring a new set back from London. It was during this trip that he dropped in on Floyd at the 'See Emily Play' sessions and first saw the dramatic change in Syd.

Shrugging off the unsettling encounter, Gilmour's thoughts returned to his Jokers Wild colleagues stranded in a foreign country without food or money. Catching the boat train back to

Paris he returned with the precious microphones and Jokers Wild resumed their interpretations of current chart sounds to somewhat disinterested French audiences for another six months.

Gilmour: "The whole thing eventually disintegrated into aggravation and we did a last 'GBH' tour of the clubs that hadn't paid us – going round to everyone's office in a show of muscular force, stealing things and threatening them with violence if they didn't cough up what they owed us.

"We finally headed back to England with no money at all. We couldn't find a petrol station so we had to steal some diesel off a building site to keep the van going until it reached the ferry. Unfortunately it was a petrol van which didn't like diesel very much so we had to keep the engine running all the time to prevent it from cutting out. We ended up keeping it running for six hours while we waited in the car park for the ferry. We managed to drive it on board but had to push it off when we arrived in England."

Gilmour was to discover that the French have long memories. Years later he returned as a rich rock star to the scene of his near starvation and had the bad luck to check into the same Paris hotel he'd left without paying his bill in 1967. The manager was unimpressed by the guitarist's new-found celebrity status and made him settle the outstanding account on the spot.

For Gilmour's bedraggled outfit, the return to England was equivalent to the retreat from Dunkirk – a sense of failure heightened by Pink Floyd's burgeoning success. Their arrival coincided with the release of 'Apples And Oranges'. For Wills and Wilson at least, the pop world had temporarily lost much of its attraction. It wasn't the end of their association with Gilmour – he recruited them for his eponymous first solo LP in 1978 – but for now the weary duo headed sheepishly back to their parents' homes in Cambridge while the more resilient Gilmour moved into a seedy Fulham bed-sit whose landlord was dubbed 'Mad Morag'.

Gilmour still wasn't particularly friendly with Syd's Floyd colleagues, having only met them a handful of times, but when he attended a London gig at Christmas, Nick Mason sidled up and suggested the band would be in touch fairly soon. Pressed for an explanation, Mason replied enigmatically: "Things are on the move . . . we can't handle it any longer."

Just after New Year, the telephone rang in Gilmour's Fulham flat. It was Nigel Lesmoire-Gordon who breathlessly told him: "Dave (dramatic pause), this could be the biggest moment of your life . . ."

Gilmour: "He said they wanted me to join the band and told me to ring Jenner and King. I thought I could probably help knock the band into shape. I think they chose me because I came from a similar background and they probably thought they would get along with me."

Waters and Mason did not mince words at the meeting when it was agreed to bring in Gilmour and put him on £7 a week. They bluntly told him Syd was mad and they couldn't carry on with him.

Gilmour: "The idea was to let me play guitar and sing on the records and Syd would be left to waffle on on his own. There was another plan that he could stay home and write stuff but not be allowed to come out on stage and ruin gigs every night. It seemed to change every five minutes. At this point the band were dying a death everywhere. The only places where they could carry on were venues like UFO and Middle Earth where every one was so out of their brains that the weirder it was, the better they liked it.

"It wasn't impossible to play with Syd – it was totally impossible. It was a purely practical decision. There was no other choice left. If he'd stayed, the Floyd would have died an ignominious death."

Over the years there have been suggestions that Syd's colleagues took advantage of his condition to oust him from the group. Gilmour frankly admits that there is an element of truth in this: "The fact is that people in rock 'n' roll bands want to succeed very much and when they achieve a certain degree of success and see that being sucked away from them, they're going to get ruthless. You have to come up with decisions that are tough for you to make and tough for other people to take."

He dismisses any suggestion that by replacing Barrett he was put in an uncomfortable position. "I don't think I even considered Syd would know it had happened. He was so way out at the time. Normally we would pick him up in the Bentley but one day someone asked: 'Shall we pick Syd up?' and someone else replied: 'No, let's not bother.' We never went to pick him up again. It's as simple as that."

The ousting of the band's leader has never before been described in such chilling matter-of-fact tones. The rest of the Floyd had come to regard Barrett as a liability and must have been reassured by Gilmour's down-to-earth presence. But if they thought Syd would meekly accept that his Floydian days were over, they were badly mistaken. He still had the group schedule and on a number of occasions he was glimpsed standing silently in the audience. At this stage Gilmour did begin to feel some discomfort. One unsettling incident was at Middle Earth soon after the break had been made official.

Gilmour: "Syd came in and stood right in front of me. I was at the front of the stage so his head would have been at about my foot height. He stood there looking up at the microphone glaring at me all the way through."

Gilmour's grim experiences on the Continent proved he was no quitter. Nevertheless, he was profoundly disturbed by Syd's obvious show of malevolence, telling his flatmate Ian Moore: "I don't think I can take much more." The animosity towards the guitarist was not to be repeated but Syd's violent behaviour towards Lynsey had become more serious.

They had moved in with friends in Richmond but the couple they chose as minders were a pair of fast-living LSD freaks known as Mad Jock and Mad Sue who had been on the fringes of the Floyd scene for some time. Considering their reputation, the decision was like asking an alcoholic to run a brewery. Sue and Jock's peculiar idea of hospitality was spiking their guests' morning coffee with large doses of acid. Consequently when Storm Thorgeson next ran into Syd, he discovered he had 'tripped' solidly for three months without realising it. Thorgeson immediately took Syd and Lynsey back to his own South Kensington flat.

Thorgeson: "He was pretty uncommunicative – all right some days and worse on others – he was violent towards Lynsey but not towards us. On one occasion I had to pull him off Lynsey because he was beating her over the head with a mandolin."

In May, Pete Jenner took Syd back into the studio for a stab at recording some solo tracks. After a week he was forced to admit defeat. "I had seriously underestimated the difficulties of working with him," he says.

Shortly after this, Syd broke up with Lynsey and, fuelled by LSD and large doses of mandrax pills, set out on a wild drive around Britain in his Mini. The jaunt ended back in Cambridge where he received psychiatric treatment at the local hospital where a number of local acid casualties had already been treated.

One memorable event from this critical period in Syd's life graphically illustrates how his unorthodox behaviour added to the legend. It has become known as the 'mandrax incident' and reportedly took place at one of his last gigs with Pink Floyd. The venue is unknown, but it appears to have happened when the rest of the band had walked on stage leaving Barrett alone in the dressing room frantically trying to arrange his tousled head of hair. As a last resort, and more through desperation than anything, he poured his coloured mandrax pills into a jar of Brylcreem and slopped the entire mess on his head. Picking up his guitar, he strode purposefully on stage.

Underneath the hot lights the coagulated gunge began to melt and drip down over Syd's forehead, and a couple of dozen freaked out fans in the front row screamed in unison as his face looked for all the world as if it was disintegrating before their very eyes.

Chapter Seven

The Madcap Laughs

A fter a short spell in hospital, Barrett was once more drawn to London where he set about making a public comeback. His first task was to find a flat and he eventually settled for a three-room apartment in exclusive Earls Court Square. Just before Christmas 1968, he moved in with two flatmates. One left almost immediately, the other was the now successful pop artist Duggie Fields.

At the time Fields was a 23-year-old student at the Regent Street Polytechnic, who had been introduced into the Floyd entourage by Rick Wright's wife Juliette. After college, Fields spent a year in America but on returning he quickly renewed contact with former acquaintances in London and towards the end of the year Syd wondered if he might like to share a flat. Fields, then enduring a miserable existence in a dank Holland Road basement, needed no second invitation, though he was later to have second thoughts about the decision.

Fields discovered the flat that would later feature on the cover of 'The Madcap Laughs', but it was the more affluent Barrett who signed the lease. By chance, the new pad was situated next to Gilmour's flat and Barrett's Floyd successor could see right into The Madcap's kitchen.

Right from the start, the artist in Syd was in obvious competition with Fields and to visitors it sometimes appeared that the two were involved in some sort of bizarre race. While Fields worked studiously on his latest painting, Barrett toiled in the next room, conjuring up vivid creations from his own mind but seemingly never able to finish anything.

One semi-completed work was of a dark castle, another was a curious wire, paper and silk model which hung from the ceiling.

Fields, who quickly sensed the ego clash, began to doubt Syd's motivation: "You have to have some reason for doing things – usually money – and his money problems were taken care of by his earlier musical successes. The pressure of having to produce something to earn money was taken off him very early. When we moved in, I noticed he'd changed from the Syd I had known before moving to America. He was definitely nuttier and had become more withdrawn and moody. His deterioration was gradual until he reached the stage where he'd just lie in bed because he couldn't decide what to do. I did not rate him as an artist but perhaps he would have made it if he hadn't switched to music. He was talented but lacked direction and had no idea how to follow an idea through. He never discussed the Floyd but he did have identity problems about having been a pop star and now maybe not being one. He saw Dave (Gilmour) quite a bit. He may have been his replacement but Dave was the one he got on with for the longest time afterwards.

"To do something in a group is fine to begin with, but people change and move in different directions. The pressure of having sudden success is difficult for anyone to cope with. Things no longer seem pleasurable when you feel you must carry on repeating them and all this added to his withdrawal."

During the first few weeks in the new flat, Syd's overall state actually improved considerably and soon after settling in he was talking about a return to recording. After all, Barrett was still a respected and now greatly missed part of the London Underground and he had managed to write a handful of new songs since the split. These, along with the unfinished recordings from the earlier Pete Jenner sessions, would be the framework of his first solo album. The first task was to book studio time at EMI and he was lucky that his request reached the ears of Malcolm Jones, a recent EMI recruit who had joined straight from university.

Jones was the 23-year-old boss of Harvest, a new progressive label set up by the parent company to compete with more fashionable independent rivals. Pink Floyd would soon switch from EMI's Columbia label to Harvest and other 'progressive' rock bands signed to EMI, notably Deep Purple, would follow suit. Syd's approach was timely. Following Harvest's successful launch, the enthusiastic Jones was planning more releases to build up the label's catalogue and establish its identity in a field that was rapidly becoming overcrowded.

He had never met Syd, but Jones was familiar with his past work and by chance had already quizzed the EMI management over a possible solo career for the once prolific songwriter. Dark references were made to chaos and general disorder in studios, broken microphones and other prima donna misdemeanours. Although EMI never actually accused Syd of causing the damage, it was strongly implied that he was *persona non grata* at Abbey Road. No one at EMI was falling over themselves to welcome him back.

Undeterred, Jones was sufficiently intrigued to contact Barrett who claimed he had a wealth of material waiting to be recorded. The Harvest boss was impressed by Syd's 'togetherness' which was in stark contrast to the groundswell of rumour. Syd said there was one song called 'Opel', another called 'Terrapin', a third about an Indian girl called 'Swan Lee', and a final one with the title 'Clowns And Jugglers'. He had also started work on a James Joyce poem, 'Golden Hair', which he was most anxious to complete. To Jones, whose imagination had been fired by the many 'crazy-Syd' tales, it all seemed too good to be true.

He talked the EMI bosses into letting Syd back into the studio, pointing out that they could be missing out on a lucrative career to run alongside that of his former Floyd colleagues, presently entrenched in the recording of a soundtrack for the Barbet Schroeder film *More*.

Barrett began work at EMI's Studio Three in early April with Jones himself in the producer's chair. Although far smaller than the main studio Pink Floyd were using only a drum beat away, Jones considered it more intimate and felt Barrett would appreciate the more relaxed atmosphere: "Syd was in great mood and fine form, a stark contrast to the rumours I'd been fed with. In little over five hours we'd laid down vocal and guitar tracks for four new songs and two old ones. At Syd's request, the first thing we did was 'Opel'. We both felt at the time it was one of his best new songs. Syd took nine runs at it to get a complete take, but nevertheless it had a stark attraction to it."

By midnight Jones and Barrett had worked on seven titles and felt they had done enough for one day. On the way home in a cab Syd said he'd be bringing some backing musicians for the next session. One of these was drummer Jerry Shirley. He had arrived in London at the age of 16 after landing a job with Steve Marriott's Humble Pie. He lived close to Barrett and was keen to play on the album. Shirley frequently visited Barrett's apartment and recalls it vividly: "That flat was an absolute hovel, although originally it had been a very fine apartment. It was your typical hippy-type hangout – washing-up never done, dog shit in the corner, cat piss on the floor and Sunday papers all over the place. In those days most people's flats looked like that but Syd's was particularly raunchy."

The teenage Shirley, new to London and somewhat over-awed by the whole scene, found Syd rather unnerving: "You could have a perfectly normal conversation with him for half-an-hour then he would suddenly switch off and his mind would go off somewhere else. One night I went down to The Speakeasy with him and on the way he was quite all right, chatty and absolutely normal. We walked in and there was this instant pressure of people looking at Syd – not that it would have seemed like that to most people – and he absolutely froze, wouldn't say a word.

"Syd had a terrible habit of looking at you and laughing in a way that made you feel really stupid. He gave the impression he knew something you didn't. He had this manic sort of giggle which made 'The Madcap Laughs' such an appropriate name for his album – he really did laugh at you."

Shirley and Willie Wilson, the former Jokers Wild drummer, were both drafted into the making of the LP midway through April, helping in the recording of 'No Man's Land', with its bizarre incoherent spoken piece, and 'Here I Go', the second 'old timey' song on the album. Jones states categorically that this latter track, with its unusual music hall structure, was written in the studio in a matter of minutes, so refuting Roger Waters' assertion that all Syd's material was written prior to the split with Pink Floyd. The track was recorded 'live' with the freshly written lyrics in front of Syd.

"He used to read his lyrics off a stand. If someone knew a song well enough, I wouldn't have thought it necessary to start reading the words off a stand two years later," says Jones.

Dave Gilmour also maintains that songs such as 'Rats' and 'Maisie' on the second album simply fell into place during studio rehearsals. Barrett never had eye contact with fellow musicians in the studio as everyone would face the control room and watch him from behind. Syd rarely issued instructions on how to play a song so the others simply adopted a policy of trial and error – a situation that proved murderously difficult but one that they handled quite well in the circumstances.

Jones: "It was a case of following him, not playing with him. There was no togetherness because they were always backing musicians to Syd and not a group. They were seeing and then playing so they were always a note behind."

As far as Jerry Shirley was concerned, Barrett's behaviour in the studio was exactly the same as outside.

"He'd let everyone else get on with it or try to explain what he wanted and get nowhere, then he'd suddenly come out with this crystal clear statement. When this happened he seemed as normal as the next chap and I wondered whether he was just testing us. He possibly knew something was happening to him and used everyone around him to play mind games."

Syd turned up at one session clutching a small portable cassette player which Jones assumed he had brought to make a copy of a long and tedious track called 'Rhamadan', recorded by Jenner the previous May. Instead, he said he wanted to overdub some motorbike sounds onto the track and had been out on the back of a friend's bike with the recorder. Jones was dismayed when Syd played him the cassette. Not only was the quality poor but there was no starting or revving sound – Syd had recorded just one long continuous note. Although the producer dug up a motorbike tape from EMI's large sound effects library, he never found out what Syd had planned as he later changed his mind and abandoned the exercise.

The following month, various members of Soft Machine tackled the difficult task of overdubbing on Syd's ragged and unpredictable tracks. The group's Robert Wyatt thought the sessions were merely rehearsals for the real thing. "We'd say, 'What key is that in Syd?' And he would simply reply: 'Yeah!' or 'That's funny'."

Ironically the quirky nature of 'The Madcap' songs is the very thing that endears them to many Barrett fans.

When Syd transferred all the four-tracks to eight-track for the final mixing, Jones noticed that 'Opel' was among them: "Syd obviously intended to include it on the album. I still think to this day that it is one of his best tracks and it's tragic that it wasn't included on the final album."

By now the Floyd had completed the soundtrack to *More* and following a meeting with Syd at Waters' Shepherds Bush flat they agreed to speed up production of 'Madcap' by taking on the remaining tracks themselves. They supervised the remaking of 'Clowns And Jugglers' – with the new title 'Octopus' – and 'Golden Hair', which had developed into one of Syd's finest solo efforts, plus two new titles, 'Dark Globe' and 'Long Gone'. Waters and Gilmour then returned to complete work on the third Floyd album 'Ummagumma' which, coupled with a short tour of Holland, meant the final touches to Syd's album were postponed until late July. Syd was understandably frustrated by the delay and decided to take a holiday, following a large crowd of Cambridge hippies who had jetted off to the Mediterranean island of Ibiza.

Among them was Ian Moore: "One day we decided to go into San Fernando on Ibiza and saw a strange figure across the square who looked exactly like Syd. He was standing there smiling at us in his bright satin shirt, velvet trousers and Gohills boots. It couldn't have been anyone else – Syd often visited our London flat and when he realised we'd left without him he made a girlfriend book him a flight and drive him to the airport."

Dealing with the inconvenience of check-in desks, customs and ticket barriers was not high on the list of Barrett priorities. Late for his plane, he skipped the lot, ran towards the runway and tried to flag down a passing jet as if it were a cab. Syd, who'd told his flatmate he was merely popping out "for an afternoon drive" duly arrived in the Mediterranean a few hours later and crossed the square to greet his amazed friends with a non-chalant: "Hi."

Moore: "He had a carrier bag of clothes that I could smell from where I was standing. The bag was full of money – he had gone to his London bank and taken out a load of cash but had forgotten to change it when he arrived in Spain."

Syd's bright garb was no particular surprise to the plainly-clothed locals that summer, as it seemed that the entire Kings Road set had forsaken the grime of the city for sand, sea and sex in the sun.

Moore: "We had all taken our Chelsea clothes with us but we were totally out of place on Ibiza so we decided to move *en masse* to Formentaire – the lesser-known island next door. Syd was still great to be with and we had some amazing times when he would play the guitar or come down to the beach with us. He would be laughing and telling us a joke one minute and then suddenly go back to his land of never-never. Although the sun was extremely hot he didn't take much care of his body. We continually told him to cover up but he wouldn't take any notice and ended up suffering third degree burns. Blisters came up all over his body and burst on his chest and back making his shirts stick to his skin. In the end we had to grab him, hold him down, and cover him from head to toe in Nivea."

Back in London, work on the album moved into its final phase. According to Gilmour, EMI was becoming increasingly worried about a project it had spent a considerable amount of money on without seeing any return. He believes the record company was considering shelving the album when Barrett approached him and Waters for help in finishing it.

The last 'Madcap' session took place on July 26 and included the segued section 'She Took A Long Cold Look', 'Feel', and 'If It's In You'.

Gilmour: "EMI gave us two days' recording time. On one of those days we had a gig and had to leave at 5.30 in the afternoon. We recorded the rest of the album in a day-and-a-half. I did all the mixing, trying to make sense of it with varying degrees of success. At least we got the album out – EMI had spent a lot of money on something it thought wasn't going to happen."

The rushed final recording session reveals a very different Syd from the one who had been sufficiently together to record and mix the first 'Madcap' tracks in the spring. What happened in the studio that day would lead one writer to describe the album as "a portrait of a breakdown." Syd falters during 'She Took A Long Cold Look' and the turning of his lyric pages can clearly be heard. Singing in a tortured voice, he launches into 'Feel' with no accompaniment from his guitar. During the closing 'If It's In You' he finally breaks down and has to restart. Syd just couldn't find the right key to the song which, more than any other, prompted *Melody Maker* to describe the album as "the mayhem and madness representing the Barrett mind unleashed."

Over the years, these anguished pieces have aroused considerable controversy. Was it really necessary to include them and why was the classic 'Opel' omitted, remaining unreleased until the rarities album of 1988?

Jones: "When I first heard the finished product it came as a shock. This wasn't the Syd of two or three months ago. I felt angry. It's like dirty linen in public and very unnecessary and unkind. Keeping conversation in is all very well if it enhances the record but I fail to see how the sound of pages being turned can do anything for Syd, I fail to see the point."

Gilmour also regrets this part of the album which, given another chance, he'd do differently. "It's very hard to say whether one's decisions are the right ones or the wrong ones but those are the decisions we made. We wanted to inject some honesty into it to try and explain what was going on. We didn't want to appear cruel but there is one bit I wish I hadn't done in retrospect. Don't forget we were digging around for stuff to put on the album. Syd wanted to do one song called 'Two Of A Kind' which Rick (Wright) wrote. He thought it was his!"

Questioned about the exclusion of 'Opel', Gilmour cannot remember the track and wrongly assumes it to be an alternative title for one of the released songs. Sadly, it appears that during the undignified scramble of the final recording and mixing, this classic Barrett track was overlooked.

The task of designing the album sleeve fell to Storm Thorgeson and his partner Aubrey 'Po' Powell at Hipgnosis. That October Malcolm Jones dropped into Syd's flat to leave a tape of the album and what he saw gave him quite a start: "In anticipation of the photographic session Syd had painted the floorboards of his room orange and purple. Up until then the floor had been bare with Syd's possessions mostly on the floor – hi-fi, guitar, cushions, books and paintings. Syd was well pleased with his day's work and I must say it made a fine setting for the session due to take place."

By the time the art work was completed it was too late to have the album pressed and into the shops in time for Christmas. Realising there was still a fair amount of money around in January, Harvest delayed release until late that month, selecting 'Octopus' backed with 'Golden Hair' as a single to promote it.

Initial reaction was favourable although, apart from a live session on *Top Gear*, there was precious little airplay for either single or album. EMI was still half-hearted towards Harvest and the only person who played Syd on the radio was John Peel. Radio was even more chart orientated than it is today but even so a sales figures sheet at the end of February showed 'The Madcap Laughs' had sold over 6,000 copies, mainly through word-of-mouth based on Barrett's reputation.

Disc announced that it was "an excellent album to start 1970" while *Beat Instrumental* labelled it a beautiful solo record, best played late at night. The January 31 edition of *Melody Maker* carried a slightly rambling interview with Syd saying *Top Of The Pops* was all right. He claimed to have written lots more material and EMI decided that public response was sufficiently enthusiastic to warrant the making of a second album. Sessions started almost immediately, on February 26.

In an *NME* interview with Richard Green on March 14, Syd explained how he'd spent a year "resting and getting the album together." The next step, he said, would be a new band and album: "Making my own album was fine because after two years away from the group I didn't have to lead on from anywhere. I want to discover now if it's possible to continue some of the ideas that come from a couple of tracks on the first album."

The follow-up album 'Barrett' had Gilmour back in the producer's chair, Rick Wright on keyboards and Jerry Shirley on drums.

Gilmour: "This time we had the chance of making an album from beginning to end but we were still faced with the inescapable fact that there were two ways of recording Syd. One was to make a backing track and get him to play along with it – which lost an elementary part of what Syd did; the other was to put Syd down first and add everyone else on afterwards – which loses the factor of basic togetherness. Either way, it was murder."

Critics agree that while tracks like 'Baby Lemonade' and 'Gigolo Aunt' are crisp and clear, they lose an essential part of Barrett. On the other hand, 'Rats' was recorded with Syd playing a guitar and everyone else added afterwards. Even Gilmour admits: "It's got the mayhem and the madness of Syd and it's great."

Syd himself had little to say about the album: "There'll be all kinds of things. It just depends on what I feel like doing at the time. The important thing is that it will be better than the last. There are no set musicians, just people helping out like on 'Madcap' which gives me far more freedom in what I want to do."

Shirley: "Sometimes Syd couldn't play anything that made sense, other times what he'd play was absolute magic. He would never play the same tune twice. 'Baby Lemonade' had been recorded without drums and Dave called me in to overdub some. He had to stand in front of me and conduct because it had no musical direction – maybe that's why people like it."

Syd's confused instructions were impossible to follow. He would describe musical passages in abstract ways, almost as if he were describing one of his paintings. "Perhaps we could make the middle darker and maybe the end a bit middle afternoonish," he'd say. "At the moment it's too windy and icy."

During the making of 'Barrett', Syd made his first stage appearance since leaving the Floyd two-and-a-half years earlier. The occasion was the *Olympia Extravaganza* in early June when he performed four numbers with Gilmour on bass and Shirley on drums. Syd initially begged the others to go along with the idea but in the end he had to be cajoled into doing it himself owing to last-minute stage fright. Just before his entrance, Barrett could be seen peeping fearfully from behind the curtain at the expectant crowd, terrified at the prospect of performing live.

Against all odds the gig actually went well. Encouraged by the large audience, Barrett, Gilmour and Shirley raced through four numbers at breakneck speed before Syd abruptly ended proceedings with a mumbled "Thank you and goodnight." His unexpected exit took Gilmour and Shirley completely by surprise.

When it appeared, the album sleeve was bedecked with insect sketches drawn by Barrett in his Cambridge Art School days. The sleeve may be significant for reasons which have previously never been aired. On closer inspection, the winged insects all appear to be beetles. Syd's fixation with John Lennon was well known. Could this have been a tribute to his favourite group, and a hint that now he once again regarded himself as an artist?

Back at the Earls Court flat, the atmosphere had become more strained and the rows more intense and frequent. Duggie Fields had noticed Syd's further disintegration: "He had these green hessian curtains in his room. One day he came home with some mcre which he pinned over the green ones to stop the daylight filtering in while he lay in bed most of the day. This effectively meant he couldn't open the windows so gradually the smell wafting out of the room became unbearable. He used to lock himself in, but when he went to the bathroom I'd nip inside to open a window and let in some fresh air."

Inevitably this situation began to cause considerable friction and Fields finally indicated his growing displeasure by refusing to speak to his flatmate or keep checking up on him. He was forced to regret the tactic when Syd attempted to cook a meal on the flat's primitive electric cooker.

"By this time I was getting really paranoid so when I smelled burning I was determined not to check up on him. Eventually the smell became so unbelievably strong that I just couldn't bear it. The hall was a cloud of black smoke and I had trouble finding my way to the kitchen. I found that Syd had put on some oil to cook chips and had just left it. The oil had evaporated, the handle of the pan had started to melt and the whole room from wall to ceiling was black. He'd put the fire out and just walked into his room with a laugh.

"I did try to cope with his behavioural problems but it reached the stage where just going out with him was an ordeal. It was like being with a child – you had to tell him when to cross the road and when to turn down a street. Once we reached our destination he'd sometimes sit there and not say a word until it was time to go again. After a while I just didn't want to do it."

Syd's state wasn't helped by the endless stream of hangers-on, drug-pushers, and groupies he always seemed to attract. Fields never saw Barrett take acid but the flat was seldom without hash, grass, speed and various forms of downers. As if life wasn't chaotic enough, the scene was worsened by the arrival of a hippie couple named Rusty and Greta who, having nowhere to live, camped in the hall, sharing large amounts of speed and mandrax.

Syd was still physically attractive and most girls instantly fancied him. After the split with Lynsey, he threw himself into a string of casual affairs. Fields: "The girl who appeared naked on the cover of 'The Madcap Laughs' was a half-Eskimo called Iggy who was destitute when she came to see us. She had a heavy period and always seemed to be wrapped in bloodstained towels. She often wore a gold, forties-style dress which went to the ground and had a train tied up to the wrist. It was slightly see-through and she never had any underwear on. Once I recall seeing her getting off a bus wearing a scarf as a skirt."

Syd's behaviour was occasionally punctuated with the acts of violence that had characterised his final days with Lynsey. Fields: "One Sunday a group of us, including a girlfriend of Syd's called Gilly, decided to go round and see Dave Gilmour. Gilly then changed her mind and lay down on Syd's bed. He told her it was his room and she had to go, then he just picked her up and threw her across the room. She literally went through the air and landed at our feet – we were all speechless. She wasn't turned off by that though. Another girl called Lesley was also very keen on Syd and visited a lot. Sometimes he'd let her in and other times he'd just shut himself in his room leaving her in the hallway banging on his door. Once he spent the night with her but threw her out the next day. She was back for more afterwards as well."

Despite the steady stream of admirers that came his way, there were only three major relationships in Syd's life – his schoolboy romance with Libby Gausden, the tempestuous relationship with Lynsey, and his love affair with Gayla Pinion.

Gayla, like Syd's other close girlfriends, was a Cambridge girl who came from Ely, a small town about 20 miles out of the city. She was a friend of Lynsey's and it was through her that she had first met Syd when the pair were living at Egerton Court in 1968. Towards the end of the next year, 19-year-old Gayla had moved to London intent on becoming a model. The vivacious teenager with flaming red hair was staying with 'Po' Powell when she first caught Barrett's eye.

He would sometimes turn up at Powell's flat first thing in the morning or last thing at night, always on the pretence of seeing Po. It was clear to all that Gayla was becoming an obsession and Syd's desire was not unrequited, as Gayla recalls: "Syd was very good-looking and had this sort of mad attractiveness about him. He had the most extraordinary eyes and when he looked at you, you felt hopelessly caught."

The rather green Cambridge teenager had arrived in London with just her savings and a West Highland Terrier called Sasha

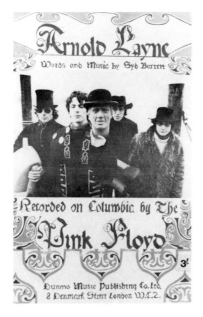 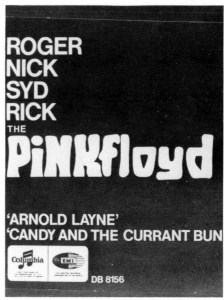

Left: The original sheet music for Syd's *Arnold Layne*. Right: an advert for the single.

Pink Floyd, 1967. Left to right: Rick, Roger, Nick and Syd. *(Phtographer unknown)*

Syd with friends at Cambridge, 1966, including Lynsey Korner (wearing sunglasses). Syd is second from right. *(Ian Moore Collection)*

Syd on holiday in Greece, 1969, with unknown girl. *(Ian Moore Collection)*

Early paintings by Syd Barrett. *(Barrett Family Collection)*

Syd, (far right), with Pink Floyd in a group photo with touring colleagues, including The Jimi Hendrix Experience, The Move and Amen Corner. *(Photographer unknown)*

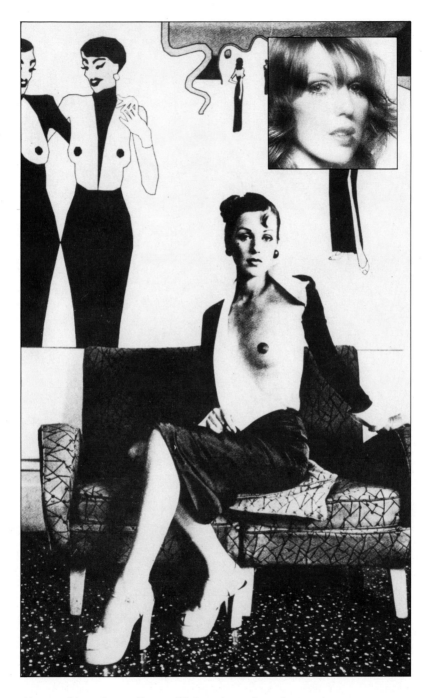

Above and inset: Lynsey Korner. *(Photographers unknown)*

Pink Floyd enter Gothic territory towards the end of Syd's tenure with the band.
(Photographer unknown)

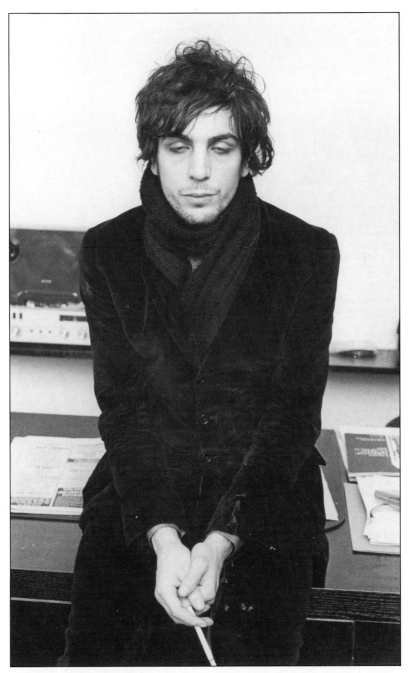

Syd in 1971. *(Barry Plummer)*

Above: Syd in 1978. *(Barrett Family Collection)* Inset: Syd, at a Garden fete in Cambridge in 1981, with sister Rosemary (left) and mother Winifred (right). *(Barrett Family Collection)*

Syd photographed in Cambridge in September, 1989. *(Bob Seymore)*

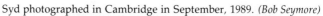

which became a major stumbling block in the blossoming romance. Syd hated the dog – probably because it took Gayla's attention away from him.

Gayla took a job in The Chelsea Drug Store and three months later moved into Syd and Duggie's living room. To Gayla it seemed that her new boyfriend was still torn between being a pop star and an artist and was clearly jealous of Fields who now diligently avoided him by painting in his room all day.

"Syd would lock himself in his room and paint all night. Even at that point he had reclusive tendencies. He used to torment me about Lynsey. He was like two people – one moment so kind and so loving and then he'd change completely. Sometimes, in the middle of the night, he'd walk all the way to Battersea to see friends and arrive at three am completely out of his tree. Being Syd Barrett he was always welcomed with open arms. He was still a star and people treated him like one."

Syd's pent-up frustration frequently boiled over into violence and Gayla was usually on the receiving end. She was a robust girl capable of fighting back and the luckless Fields was once hurt trying to separate them. On another occasion, Syd hurled a milk bottle at Gayla, who ducked. The gold-top missile crashed into and damaged one of Field's paintings.

Gayla: "In the summer I went for a holiday in Jersey with Lynsey. When I came back Syd was overjoyed to see me but within half-an-hour he had changed. He was always strange when she was there and just used to sit on the bed and stare at her."

The unpleasant atmosphere cleared for a short time during the making of 'Barrett' when he would often ask Gayla and Duggie for an opinion on the music.

During that summer of 1970, as Pink Floyd toiled on their latest LP 'Atom Heart Mother' in Abbey Road Studios, Roger Waters had a puzzling encounter with Syd in Harrods department store in Knightsbridge. Waters was apparently browsing round the upmarket shop when he suddenly spotted Syd walking towards him, a large Harrods bag in each hand. As soon as their eyes met Syd dropped the bags and raced outside, leaving a perplexed Waters behind him. Going over to inspect the bags, Waters found hundreds of children's sweets. He was left standing helplessly in the middle of Harrods wondering what he could do with the countless sherbets, fruit drops and humbugs.

Around this time Syd also had an encounter with his old Cambridge mate Geoff Mott, who was still playing with The Boston Crabs. In London one night with nowhere to stay, Mott called at Syd's flat. The following morning he heard Syd playing a haunting little tune on his Fender and asked for the lyrics. It turned out to be 'Wined And Dined', a song which would appear on the 'Barrett' album and one apparently written about Gayla.

Later that day Syd took Mott to Abbey Road to spy on the Floyd sessions. Mott: "I found it rather sad although there was nothing sad about Syd's behaviour. I can still see him keeping an eye on proceedings, sitting on his hands with that quizzical smile on his face."

There was very little for Gayla to smile about. Unable to cope with the worst excesses of Syd's behaviour, she fled to her parents' home in Ely. When she telephoned Fields, he reported that Syd was locked in his room, brooding. People closest to Barrett noticed he was becoming more reclusive and now seldom ventured out of the flat. The crowd of hangers-on had increased, along with the amounts of drugs they brought with them. Fields, furious with the unwanted intrusion, stubbornly locked himself away in his own room but could not escape the sound of girls crying and pleading with Syd to open his door.

Fields: "They might have been using him for money and I think he got fed up with it. He started going back to Cambridge for longer and longer periods and left me with a house full of people. He then had the nerve to ask me to get rid of them and I later found out that he'd tried to make out I was the bad guy responsible."

Syd's relationship with Gayla continued as a series of violent arguments interspersed with loving reconciliations. On one occasion he proved a tower of strength during a crisis at the Pinion home. Gayla: "He came down to see me and was kindness itself. I couldn't help laughing at my mother's face when she saw him waiting to catch the bus back to Cambridge. He was standing there in the pouring rain in his pop star clothes. Being Syd he hadn't considered using the bus shelter."

Gayla also noticed that Syd had tired of London life and was more interested in a return to his past Cambridge days. On one trip to see his mother he announced that he and Gayla would be moving back there to live. Although the 'Barrett' album was due for release in November, Syd showed no enthusiasm for promoting it. Instead he told astonished friends he was going to marry Gayla, become a medical student and qualify as a doctor.

In many ways Syd drove himself out of his London flat. Fields was no longer talking to him and the squatters made life unbearable. Gayla finally persuaded him to hand over the lease to Duggie before they disappeared back to Cambridge – a sane island in a sea of madness. Barrett simply locked his room, leaving all his possessions inside and shut the door on another chapter of his life.

Chapter Eight

Full Of Dust And Guitars

Six years after leaving Cambridge for Camberwell Art College, Syd returned to 183 Hills Road with Gayla in tow. They moved into the basement den of his mother's home which she had kept exactly as Syd had left it back in 1964. While he took comfort from the familiar surroundings of his boyhood retreat – his paintings, books and maternal support – Gayla took a job in a local furniture store. The set-up immediately ran into problems when Syd heard that Gayla's old boyfriend worked in the bed department. He suspected they were having an affair and insisted on walking her to and from work every day. Syd's jealousy reached the point where Gayla often found him lurking behind shelves in the store in order to keep a watchful eye on her until her shift ended.

Syd seemed to be torn between anonymity and recognition. He studiously ignored the student lodgers at his mother's house but occasionally visited Andy's Record Store where he knew he was guaranteed undivided attention.

Gayla: "We were engaged on October 1, 1970, my 20th birthday. His mother was all for it and my parents were invited over for a celebration meal. It was just like a normal engagement in some ways. He bought a ring and his mother put an announcement in the local paper. Then there was this mad obsession with finding somewhere to live. When we went to see flats he was always embarrassed and tongue-tied and it was me who ended up doing most of the talking. Then he'd ruin it when our prospective landlords asked him about future plans: 'I want to be a doctor,' he'd say, standing there in his Granny Takes A Trip clothes. By now I felt I was his strength. I would very much have liked to settle down and marry but he grew steadily more manic."

Mrs Barrett's fervent hope of seeing Syd married off was hardly surprising. She naturally wished that at 24 her son would settle down and forget the pop business which had already taken such a terrible toll on him. After meeting Gayla's parents, she invited the whole Barrett family to Cambridge for a celebration meal together. It was a memorable night, but for all the wrong reasons.

Gayla: "There we were sitting round the table, surrounded by these terribly normal and respectable middle-class people. We were half way through the first course when Syd suddenly coughed and spluttered, left his soup and went upstairs. When he came down, I looked up and saw that he had chopped off all his hair. And would you believe it, no one batted an eyelid. They just carried on with the meal as if nothing had happened – didn't say a word. I thought: 'Are they mad or is it me?'"

The engagement was not destined to last long. According to Gayla, Syd's violence increased and Mrs Barrett had to intervene on more than one occasion. Unable to take the treatment any longer, Gayla fled once more to her parents' home in Ely. There she received a formal letter from Syd saying the engagement was off – it was signed R.K. Barrett. He must have had a sudden change of heart as the next day she received another letter saying how much he loved her and begging her to have him back. By January Gayla was in a terrible state and went to stay at Jerry Shirley's farm at Stebbing Green, Essex, to repair her shattered nerves.

After a series of lengthy telephone conversations, they decided to make a final reconciliation attempt and agreed to meet at Bishop's Stortford railway station. Gayla was shocked to discover that Syd was still sporting a skinhead cut. On the way back to the farmhouse he accused her of having an affair with Shirley and the almighty fight that followed had to be broken up by the neighbours. The engagement was off for good.

With the stormy year-long relationship over, Syd returned alone to Cambridge. At first he seemed content to carry on living in his mother's basement, light years away from the frantic London scene. Now managed by Bryan Morrison, he stayed pretty much out of sight, only occasionally resurfacing for the odd interview or sporadic doorstep chat with Dave Gilmour. Having given up his car, Syd relied exclusively on British Rail when making his rare treks away from Cambridge. Three months after the release of 'Barrett', Syd recorded a session for the BBC radio show *Sounds Of The Seventies*, playing 'Baby Lemonade', 'Dominoes' and 'Love Song'. The show's famous compère, 'whispering' Bob Harris, told listeners that he had received many inquiries about Syd's activities since the record's release and that Barrett was now busily writing songs for his next album.

Another London visit was for an interview with Steve Turner of *Beat International* who had been on the Barrett trail for some months. Turner's first attempt at an interview stalled when Syd failed to turn up. When Turner telephoned to find out what had happened, Syd accused the interviewer of not turning up and promptly slammed down the receiver. Someone at The Bryan Morrison Agency managed to talk Syd into another meeting. The interview eventually took place in April at the publisher's office in Bruton Place, above The Revolution Club. Barrett arrived wearing a purple satin jacket, stack-heeled boots and with his hair still cropped.

Turner later recalled the obvious fear in Barrett's eyes, almost as if there was a danger the interviewer would discover something he shouldn't know: "His answers were interesting. He would start off by saying something that related to my question but then began to free-associate and would soon be off in a different direction entirely."

The interview reveals a penetrating insight into Barrett's condition. Carefully avoiding parts of his background, Barrett told Turner he spent most of his time listening to records and playing his own music in the cellar.

"Cambridge is very much a place to get adjusted to. I've found it difficult. It was fairly unusual to go back because it's the home place where I used to live. It was pretty boring so I cut my hair."

His feelings switched later in the interview: "It's quite fun. It's a nice place to live really – under the ground." Syd also announced the piece of work that his fans are still waiting for – the semi-mythical 'lost' third album – and he talked about the possibility of forming a new band. "It'd be a groove," he said, considering the suggestion from Turner.

Syd admitted he was still in love with the idea of pop stardom, a job he found interesting but difficult: "It's exciting. You channel everything into one thing and it becomes the art. I don't really know if pop is an art form. I should think (it is) as much as sitting down is."

Early on in the chat, Syd had talked excitedly about coming up to London to buy a new guitar. But three years after leaving Floyd and four years after his finest work, the reality was that he had once again lapsed into virtual inactivity.

The reporter invited Barrett to share a taxi with him to a nearby music store but Syd made some excuse about having something else to do. Turner: "I'm sure the real reason was his paranoia. Months later I met him on an underground train. He acknowledged me and remembered the interview, but it's the frightened face I'll always remember. Even so, part of what he said was highly perceptive and reminiscent of the (Bob) Dylan *Playboy* interview where much of what was said was seen as a joke at the time but proved penetratingly true in retrospect."

Michael Watts of *Melody Maker* also interviewed Barrett but the conversation, he reported, was often obscure and rarely progressed in a linear fashion. The meeting again took place in Morrison's office. Photographer Barrie Wentzell took a series of shots of Syd's crew-cut look, one of which was published alongside Watts' *MM* article. In hindsight, Watts says of the encounter: "I don't think he was as zonked out then as he later became. He was not completely freaked out . . . strange, but coherent."

Syd made some telling observations on his old band: "Their choice of material was always very much to do with what they were thinking as architectural students. Rather unexciting people, I would've thought."

The article established one interesting fact – even at this stage Syd was aware of his growing Madcap legend: "I really think the whole thing is based on me being a guitarist and having done the last thing about two or three years ago in a group around England and Europe and the States and then coming back and hardly doing anything. I could be claimed as being redundant almost. I don't feel active and that my public conscience is fully satisfied."

The two interviews helped the myth around Syd Barrett to mushroom. Here was the former leader of Pink Floyd living the life of a recluse in a cellar while the group became increasingly popular with fans and critics alike. As the group's star ascended towards mega-money overdrive, so the legend of their lost leader moved into its own orbit, feeding on his continued low profile and downright oddness. Barrett's absence from the recording scene caused rumours to fly ever faster, embellished with every telling. During the summer of 1971, various London sources were saying Syd was either dead, behind bars or a vegetable.

The wild stories prompted Peter Barnes, who worked for Syd's publishing company Lupus Music, to release a statement saying a new Barrett single would be recorded in the near future with "friends in the business who are members of well-known groups." It never happened.

Syd was already the subject of growing cultism in the USA and France, as well as in Britain. That September, the American *Phonograph Record* magazine suggested "he'd freaked out over the multimedia possibilities that rock 'n' roll offers the creative artist." If nothing else, the article renewed transatlantic interest in Syd. Intrigued by the conflicting reports and anxious to solve the Barrett mystery with a definitive article, *Rolling Stone* sent a reporter to Cambridge to track down 'missing Syd'. He wrote that Syd was alive and well in his own private world and was "as confusing as ever." He did his best to translate Syd's rambling explanation of how he was "disappearing . . . avoiding most things . . . I'm treading the backward path. Mostly I just waste my time. I walk about eight miles a day. It's bound to show. But I don't know how. I'm sorry I can't speak very coherently but you know man I'm totally together. I even think I should be. I'm full of dust and guitars. The only work I have done in the last year is interviews. I'm very good at it."

The intrepid *Rolling Stone* reporter wasn't exaggerating when he described Syd as tense and ill at ease, "hollow-cheeked and pale, with eyes reflecting a permanent state of shock." He likened him to the "ghostly beauty one associates with poets of old."

Syd spent his days wandering round Cambridge, tinkering with guitars, listening to records and painting. *Rolling Stone:* "Sometimes crazy jungles of thick blobs, sometimes linear pieces. His favourite is a white semi-circle on a white canvas. In a cellar where he spends much of his time, he sits surrounded by paintings and records, his amps and guitars. He feels safe here under the ground, like a character out of one of his songs."

Syd revealed that the recently-deceased Jimi Hendrix was still his favourite musician: "Hendrix was a perfect guitarist and that's all I wanted to do as a kid – play guitar properly and jump around. But too many people got in the way. It's always been too slow for me – playing – the pace of things. I mean, I'm a fast sprinter. The trouble was, after playing in the group for a few months, I couldn't reach that point."

He spoke of his own frustration with his inertia: "I may seem to get hung-up, that's because I am frustrated work-wise, terribly. The fact is I haven't done anything this year. I've probably been chatting, explaining that away like anything. The other bit about not working is that you do get to think theoretically."

Syd had always had a phobia about his age. Aware of pressure to return to the recording studio, he became defensive and told *Rolling Stone:* "I'm only 24. I'm still young. I've got time. I think young people should have a lot of fun." He insisted he was no longer on acid but refused to talk further about drugs. Walking out into the garden, Syd stretched himself out on a wooden seat and summed up the interview perfectly: "I don't think I'm very easy to talk about. I've got a very irregular head, and I'm not anything that you think I am anyway."

Early the next year Barrett attempted to end his malaise by joining a group. He made his first live appearance in 20 months when American blues player Eddie 'Guitar' Burns appeared at King's College, Cambridge. After a solo set, Burns announced that he would now be supported by a hurriedly-assembled boogie band consisting of the man who had made Pink Floyd, together with local bass-player Jack Monck from Delivery and former Pink Fairies' drummer Twink. Syd stood quietly at the back of the stage concentrating on his black Telecaster – few of the audience knew he was there let alone realised the significance of the occasion.

The following day Monck, then married to Syd's one-time girlfriend Jenny Spires, turned up at Twink's house and during the course of the chat someone suggested roping Barrett into a proper group. They trooped round to put the idea to Syd who, although not exactly enthusiastic, nevertheless immediately invited the pair down to jam in the basement, which also served as a makeshift studio.

Twink and the 21-year-old Monck had been running a cheap Cambridge club, known as The 10p Boogie. Monck had often seen Barrett out on his lengthy daily walks: "He would have stood out anywhere because he looked so weird. He'd grown a beard and had this white face with those really black deep-set eyes. He would strut around in a very self-conscious manner not speaking to anyone."

Twink was the driving force behind the short-lived outfit which they called Stars. From the start, Monck suspected that Syd was merely going through the motions. "He never actually said: 'Yeah, this is a good idea.' He just sort of went along with it. We often used to play down in his basement which had such a low ceiling you had to stoop. It was his retreat. We did a couple of Floyd numbers and some tracks from his solo albums including 'Terrapin'. He was still pretty keen on blues and fell back on the old 12-bar stuff a lot. I knew he wasn't totally in control but I've played with quite a few people like that."

Several years later in the fanzine *Ptolemaic Terrascope*, Twink remembered the band being put together over tea and cakes at Syd's home: "We started rehearsing in the basement the next day, took all my drums round there and just started jamming. He was painting a lot as well. He stood there one day, I think it was the first day that we went to his studio, and he had all these oil paintings that he'd done. There was this big one. I was looking at it thinking how beautiful it was and Jenny said: 'I think that's just lovely Syd.' He said: 'That's for you, Jenny.' He just gave it to her. All the time that I was working with him, it was a pleasure, it really was. Eventually we needed a bigger rehearsal place so we started rehearsing in my room in Cambridge – I was living in the back of a shop – where we knocked some of Syd's songs into shape."

The band's name had been the subject of considerable debate. Twink had suggested Twink's Stars, Syd preferred Syd Barrett's Stars and, not to be left out, Monck liked the sound of Jack Monck's Stars. Eventually, egos took second place to common sense and they settled on Stars. Their début was in an East Road café and a handful of other impromptu gigs included an informal jam in the Market Square which ended only when the long arm of the law intervened.

Monck: "I always knew Syd had great natural ability but no discipline. He never practised and we hardly ever rehearsed. It was hard to know what got through to him but I think he enjoyed a couple of the small gigs we did. The spontaneous ones went pretty well and occasionally he'd relax for a few minutes and be quite happy. He really disliked people looking on him as something special. He didn't like the bad things that went with fame – like trying to live up to what he used to be."

Stars were far from ready for a major gig but word of Barrett's stage return reached the ears of promoter Steve Brink. He had booked the outrageous American group MC5 to appear at Cambridge Corn Exchange and the prospect of the legendary Syd Barrett on the same bill was too good an opportunity to miss. Twink: "If we'd had some sort of management direction then we wouldn't have done any gigs for about six months. Instead we went straight into it."

Word of Syd's comeback reached one-time Floyd colleague Chris Dennis, now back in Cambridge working as a photographer. He telephoned Syd and asked if he could take some shots of the performance: "I rang Syd's mother and explained who I was and that I wanted to take some photos. Syd then came to the phone, said: 'We don't need any photos,' and hung up."

Ex-Mottoes member Clive Welham went backstage to see Syd for the first time in years. Welham had been warned that Barrett was not very together but he was shocked when his old friend didn't even recognise him. Half-way through Stars' faltering performance, Welham was one of several disillusioned spectators who walked out.

A feeling of expectation hung round The Corn Exchange as Syd crept on stage with Twink and Monck giving encouragement behind. Although most of the audience had come to see MC5, a mixture of genuine interest and morbid curiosity held about 30 of them rooted to the spot. Some expected the set to include a number of Floyd classics and there was a strong rumour that 'See Emily Play' had been rehearsed only the day before.

Syd opened with a slow version of 'Octopus' but his modest audience registered dismay when it became obvious that the lyrics were inaudible. Undeterred, Syd carried on with 'Dark Globe', 'Gigolo Aunt', and a couple of others from the second solo LP. After 'Gigolo Aunt' Syd was heard to mumble "I don't know what that one was called."

Monck: "It was the last gig we ever played. It wasn't a complete disaster but there was a distinct mood of anticlimax in the audience over what had been billed as a local comeback. With hindsight, I suppose we knew we were never going to get anywhere with Syd. In the end we petered out but it wasn't the music that was bad, just the presentation. What the audience saw was a man disintegrating before their eyes, a piece of bad theatre, except it wasn't make believe – it was happening for real."

With the houselights switched on to reveal a pitifully shrinking audience, Barrett struggled on, seemingly oblivious to the fact that Monck was fighting a losing battle with his fading bass amp. The gig ended when Syd's right index finger began to bleed rather badly. *Melody Maker* had sent Roy Hollingworth – a keen Barrett fan – who produced a graphic description of his idol's last stand: "He played a demented solo that ran ragged lines of up to 10 minutes. His raggled hair fell over a face that fell over a guitar and seldom looked up. He changed time almost by the minute, the keys and chords made little sense. The fingers on his left hand met the frets like strangers. They formed chords, reformed them – apparently nearly got it right – and then wandered away again. Then Syd scratched his nose and let loose a very short sigh. It was like watching somebody piece together a memory that had suffered the most severe shell-shock. I don't know how much Syd Barrett remembered, but he didn't give in. Even though he lost his bassist and even though Twink couldn't share Syd's journey, Syd played on.

"The chords are out of tune and he keeps looking to his right and sort of scowling at Twink and the bassist, as though in disagreement. I stood and watched and thought he was bloody great. A girl gets up on stage and dances; he sees her, and looks fairly startled. As the clock ticked into the small hours of Friday morning, Syd retreated to the back of the stage trying to find one of those runs. He messes chords together. There is no pattern but if you think hard you can see a faint one, you can see some trailers in the sky. The large concrete floor is littered now, not with people but with their relics. Plastic cups that contained orange juice or lemon or coffee. And some squashed wholenut scones and buns. And underground papers. And Syd played on. Will anyone listen to the Madcap?"

But the Madcap apparently didn't want to be listened to any more. The following week Syd turned up at Twink's house clutching the *Melody Maker* article and announced that that was it. Twink: "He (Hollingworth) killed the band. I thought there was a possibility that something like that might happen, but it was still a shame when it did."

Roy Hollingworth had no idea that his review would affect Syd in the way that it did, and was deeply upset when, several years later, he finally learned what had happened. "It was never my intention to harm Syd because I was his biggest fan," he says today. "He was one of my heroes. I wrote about what I saw and heard as sensitively as I could and it certainly wasn't meant to be a big put down. A little piece of me died that night too."

In hindsight, Hollingworth feels that Barrett's career wouldn't have been much different whether or not *Melody Maker* had carried the review in the first place. "But on a personal level if it hurt Syd I'm very sorry. Ideally, I'd have loved it if he had made a great comeback and gone on and on and on."

All the Stars rehearsals were recorded on tape which Syd possibly still has. There's also a rumour that the Corn Exchange fiasco was recorded, but no one seems to know what happened to the tape. With their chief attraction back skulking in his cellar, Stars collapsed like a house of cards. Twink and Monck recruited a couple of replacement guitarists and rashly pushed ahead with plans for a gig at Essex University. On hearing that Barrett was no longer in the band, the promoter speedily told them exactly what to do with the new line-up, thus marking the ignoble end of Stars.

Syd was undoubtedly wounded by the *Melody Maker* review and made a futile attempt to save face by claiming Morrison had ordered him not to play further gigs on the grounds that he could destroy what little commercial value he had left. Monck, for one, felt this was merely a smoke screen to hide his shattered confidence.

Barrett never played any of his songs live again but during one of his short visits to London that summer, the persevering

Pete Jenner whisked him into Abbey Road Studios for another crack at the third album. One Jenner associate described the exercise as an abortion as Syd repeatedly overdubbed guitar part on guitar part creating a chaotic wall of noise. "He also wouldn't show anyone his lyrics, I fear because he hadn't actually written any." Jenner was dreadfully frustrated by the experience as flashes of the old Barrett emerged sporadically only to be destroyed as Syd tried to 'improve' the results. Nothing remains from the sessions.

Barrett's own state on returning to Cambridge leaves little to the imagination. His attempts at a comeback on stage and in the studio had been disastrous and his personal crisis was heightened by Pink Floyd's continued phoenix-like rise from the ashes of the '68 split. Shortly after Christmas Syd went completely haywire in his cellar, causing considerable damage to furniture and himself. He didn't actually smash his head through the roof as has been alleged, but it was an unsavoury and distressing incident which led to the police being called and another spell in hospital for Syd.

He recovered quickly and astonishingly emerged with his appetite for music momentarily restored. Midway through 1973 his agency, Circle, released the tantalising information that Syd was "biding his time, waiting until he felt he had something new to offer." It was an empty gesture as Circle then promptly went bust.

Syd did make one surprise stage appearance that summer however. Pete Brown, Jack Bruce's lyricist, travelled up to Cambridge to meet his partner, the pair having decided to play at a local hall. Brown recalls: "Jack was living in Colchester and I arrived at the hall late to find him and this band jamming on stage. Jack was on string bass and up there with him was this odd-looking guitarist playing acoustic jazz stuff. It was his short hair and straight appearance that made him stand out. Later on, during the actual performance, various poets got up to read their pieces and I dedicated mine ('Goodnight Eliza Doolittle: The Death Of Flower Power') to Syd Barrett, saying he was the guy who started that all up in England. To my surprise, this strange guitarist stood up in the audience and said: 'No I didn't.' It turned out to be him."

Jack Bruce has only a vague recollection of the incident and does not know how the "odd looking guitarist" came to be on stage. Syd presumably saw the gig advertised and decided to attend on the spur of the moment, guitar in hand. Brown had no chance to speak to Barrett who simply vanished into the night as soon as the show ended.

He was about to enter the twilight world from which he has only occasionally emerged.

Chapter Nine

Wish You Were Here

I ronically, during this period of inactivity, Barrett's personal income began to grow. The arrival of a fat royalties cheque for the Floyd compilation album 'Relics' – released in May 1971 – allowed him to stay briefly on the top floor of London's Hilton Hotel. David Bowie's version of 'See Emily Play' on his 1973 album 'Pin-Ups' coupled with the re-packaging of Floyd's first two albums as 'A Nice Pair', in December 1973, also served to increase his wealth.

Bowie was a Floyd fan during the UFO days but in a 1973 interview he said that after Syd left, "For me, there was no more Pink Floyd." His controversial version of Barrett's best known song drew a varied response from the critics. Ian McDonald of *New Musical Express* felt Bowie had ruined the song but Andrew Wood of *International Times* declared it the best track on the album, saying: "It screams of Syd Barrett." Kevin Ayers had already included a more personal Barrett tribute on his 'Bananamour' album. The song 'Oh, Wot A Dream' was about, and dedicated to, Syd and briefly available as a single. Ayers commented: "The sincerest form of flattery being imitation, it's quite deliberately sung in Syd Barrett's style. What I tried to do was get some of the feeling that's unique to him, just to show him that although we don't talk or meet, I have a certain closeness to what he's doing and can relate to it."

Once more the unwitting object of public attention, Barrett moved back to London in search of a new flat. He was bored with Cambridge and somewhat irritated by the steady stream of callers to his door. The prospect of anonymity in the big city was very appealing.

Syd plumped for a large two-bedroom flat at the exclusive Chelsea Cloisters apartment block, just off the Kings Road. While the legend around him continued to grow out of all proportion to his recorded output, he spent his days sprawled in front of a huge bubble-shaped television set which hung from the ceiling. Over the previous two years, various sources had claimed that he was 1) working part-time in a factory; 2) had tried to enrol as an architectural student; 3) was growing mushrooms in a basement; 4) was living the life of a tramp; 5) had spent two weeks busking in New York, and 6) had tried to become a Pink Floyd roadie.

The mystique surrounding Barrett led in late 1972 to the formation of The Syd Barrett International Appreciation Society which produced a magazine called *Terrapin* and had area secretaries in Britain, Canada and the United States. The society clearly had Barrett's best interests at heart, though Nick Kent of *NME* acidly described it "as trivial as it is fanatical," and Barrett never even acknowledged its existence. The society's *raison d'être* was to encourage Syd to go back into the recording studio. It folded in mid-1974 amid a series of internal squabbles which were gleefully reported by the music press. Undaunted, Bernard White, a former area secretary, formed a new society which continued to publish *Terrapin* much to the chagrin of his former associates. White, a self-styled world authority on Barrett, continues to put out the occasional edition of *Terrapin* to this day.

Barrett's cult status was neatly captured in an excellent *NME* article by Nick Kent in the spring of 1974. Kent, who professed to being obsessed by Barrett himself, told readers that such notables as Jimmy Page, Brian Eno and Kevin Ayers had long wanted to work with the man whose only regular contact with the outside world now consisted of sporadic visits to his publisher's office near Berkeley Square whenever the rent was due.

Kent wrote: "On one of his last visits, Bryan Morrison started getting insistent that Barrett write some songs. After all, demand for new Syd Barrett material is remarkably high at the moment and EMI are all set to swoop the lad, producer in tow, into the studio at any given moment. Barrett claimed that, no, he hadn't written anything but dutifully agreed to get down and produce some sort of something. His next appearance at the office occurred last week. Asked if he had written any new tunes, he replied in his usual hazy condition, hair somewhat grown out from its former scalp-shaved condition, 'No.' He then promptly disappeared again."

Morrison was strong-willed and used to getting his own way. His limited supply of patience was rapidly running out and what little remained vanished a few months later when Syd literally bit the hand that fed him. Barrett allegedly turned up at the office asking for his monthly royalty cheque. Morrison refused, claiming Syd had received it a week earlier. After several minutes haggling, the enraged Barrett vaulted over his manager's desk and bit the end of Morrison's little finger. According to singer Roy Harper, Syd actually bit off the end of Morrison's finger tip, and far-fetched as the tale sounds, it might explain why Morrison, even today, is uncharacteristically reticent on the subject of Syd.

Kent described Barrett's story as "a huge tragedy shot through with so many ludicrously comic aspects" and claimed to have heard literally hundreds of Syd yarns during the course of his investigations. Only recently, he reported, the Madcap had visited a Kings Road boutique where he tried on three vastly different sizes of the same style of trousers, professed that they all fitted perfectly, then vanished without buying any of them.

The *NME* article, and a growing awareness of a revival of interest in Syd, prompted EMI to release his two albums in a double package that summer. Storm Thorgeson suggested a rather moving cover concept showing dozens of Barrett photographs and newspaper cuttings arranged like a fan's shrine to a departed hero. EMI, however, insisted on a current photo of the fallen hero, imprisoned in self-imposed exile within Chelsea Cloisters. Thorgeson was dispatched on the difficult mission of photographing the unstable friend he had not seen for a number of years. Finding Syd was relatively easy, it was only when Thorgeson arrived at flat 902 on the ninth floor of Chelsea Cloisters that the tricky part came. Syd's response was a terse: 'Go away. I don't want a photo.' With that he slammed the door shut.

Thorgeson: "He was of course quite within his rights to resist intrusion if he didn't want it. But I got the impression he was just being fucking difficult and that really upset me."

A couple of months later, in November 1974, Jenner fared little better when he managed to coax Syd into the studio. Any lingering hope of a fruitful session disappeared when Syd arrived with a stringless guitar. A set of strings was eventually procured from Phil May of The Pretty Things but Floyd biographer Miles described how the proceedings degenerated into a grim charade: "When everything seemed in order they began. Syd had asked someone to type his lyrics to his new songs for him. This they had done using the red ribbon of the typewriter. When the sheet was handed to Syd he thought it was a bill, grabbed the guy's hand and tried to bite his fingers off. Syd was in the studio for three days. The material put down on tape was described as 'extremely weird' and had a 'strong hardly-begun feel to it.' Only the backing tracks were recorded, no vocal tracks at all, and there is some doubt as to whether Syd even bothered to turn up on the third day. The material never reached the stage where it could be mixed and consequently remains unissued."

Jenner sees the sessions as a painful exercise in futility. He had tried to play the understanding liberal but Barrett was unhappy even under Jenner's relaxed command and he frequently disappeared for brooding walks around the studio. Jenner: "The engineer used to say that if he turned right he'd be back but if he went left he'd be gone for the day. He was never wrong."

The whole experience renewed Barrett's recurring fear of the limelight. On one of his unending walks around London he was spotted by Bernard White. Thrilled at the prospect of a pavement chat with his idol, White pursued the fleeing Barrett down Regent Street until a plaintive "Please go away" stopped him in his tracks. Crestfallen, White, who had dedicated his adult life to collecting Barrett memorabilia, watched the Madcap disappear among the afternoon shoppers.

White's chance encounter was duly logged in *Terrapin's* regular 'Syd Sightings' column. The original Barrett Appreciation Society attributed its closure to "a lack of Syd" and it is ironic to consider that the fanaticism of Barrett's most loyal supporters may unintentionally have contributed to his withdrawal.

Around the same time, one of Syd's old Cambridge friends was driving along Oxford Street when he suddenly spied him loping along the pavement. Braking to a halt, the friend leapt out and scurried after the retreating figure of Syd who stonily ignored his greeting. His forward gaze did not falter, nor did he slow down. Finally the perplexed friend asked Syd where he was walking to. Barrett stopped, turned, and fixed his piercing green eyes on the pursuer. "Far further than you could possibly imagine," he said before striding off purposefully.

Chelsea Cloisters provided a welcome retreat for Syd. The impressive red-brick apartment block is situated in the quiet Chelsea hinterland, only five minutes walk from the Kings Road. Its exclusive clientèle enjoy a first class service from staff who never intrude on their privacy. One of the porters, Ronnie Salmon, witnessed Syd's bizarre behaviour over eight years. Shortly after he started work there in January 1974, one of his colleagues identified the reclusive character on the ninth floor as "Syd Barrett, the guy who used to be in Pink Floyd."

Salmon first met Barrett when he was summoned to flat 902 to remove the huge oval television that had dominated the living room and, until this moment, most of its occupant's time. Syd took him along to a sixth floor storeroom where he kept five or six guitars, numerous amps and a box containing several tapes. Barrett collected the guitars and told the startled porter he could have all that was left – tapes, amps, records and two portable televisions.

According to Salmon, the box, possibly containing tapes of the recent studio sessions, disappeared when he popped into an Oxford Street store. The hapless porter put the box down to try on some new clothes, then walked out without it. Realising his error, he hurried back to the store only to find that the box had vanished along with some of Syd's best kept secrets.

Salmon: "When I first came to know him he was slim with long hair and the colourful clothes he wore could have come straight off their first album cover. One time he called me up to his flat and showed me a Dynatron remote control television in a beautiful cabinet. He just gave it to me saying he didn't want it."

Just as buying endless guitars had been an expensive luxury a couple of years earlier, Syd was now fascinated with televisions and had half-a-dozen in his flat at one point. But he had never cared much for money or the material wealth that went with it. His attachment to personal belongings had always been transitory, and he quickly grew bored with any new 'toy'. As early as Floyd's 1967 American tour, he bought a pink Cadillac in San Francisco – and gave it away a few days later to someone he met in the street. Green with envy, Salmon's fellow porters watched with growing disbelief at the endless stream of freebies he brought down from flat 902. "The other guys couldn't work it out but Mr Barrett seemed to like me and talked to me the most."

Salmon's theory later proved unfounded when Syd began handing out giveaways to all and sundry. One porter received some hi-fi equipment and a third got yet another discarded television. When a delivery man brought round a state-of-the-art Dynatron sound system, he was given a £300 tip and told to share it with his friends.

Salmon: "He used to buy things and then throw them away. He gave his guitars away to friends – really beautiful Fender Stratocasters. One day he walked out of the foyer with a Harrods bag and I followed him down Sloane Avenue. He threw it in a dustbin and I was curious to see what it was. It turned out to be a brand new clock radio worth £100. He used to buy suits and shirts one day and throw them away the next. He was a nice guy and usually seemed in a happy frame of mind. He had a fair bit of mail and quite a few visitors including people from the music business."

Even in this relatively tranquil period, the darker side of Syd's nature occasionally broke through. Salmon: "Once he smashed the door of his flat off its hinges. I think he was 'high' a lot of the time. His mind was there – and yet it wasn't."

Syd's eccentricity also surfaced from time to time such as when he appeared before Salmon in the foyer wearing a dress, his head newly shaven.

"He had on a Crombie coat with a dress underneath and a pair of plimsolls. I ran after him because I couldn't believe what I'd seen, and there he was walking down Sloane Avenue." Syd had brought 'Arnold Layne' to life and the disarming display no doubt appealed to his creator's dark sense of humour.

Back in the real world, Pete Jenner was suffering pangs of guilt about Syd's demise but publicly declared his continued faith in him. He told a Canadian radio interviewer that Syd's talent was still there but his songs were sketches rather than paintings: "He's a great artist, an incredibly creative artist and it's tragic that the music business may well have a lot to do with doing him in. I think we have a lot to answer for – myself and everyone else involved with him."

During this period Syd decided on a change of image. One day he stunned Chelsea Cloisters staff by arriving down in the foyer without any hair. When it grew back he took to cutting and bleaching it himself.

Salmon: "He used to drink in The Marlborough (public house) just round the corner and went from slim to fat. He became really bloated within a matter of months because he was drinking Guinness all the time. When I used to go round for a few beers with my mates, we'd see him sitting over in the corner as if in a dream. He was on his own all the time . . . always on his own. I'd try and get him to talk about his music but he just wasn't interested."

Although Syd showed no interest in his own music, he had a celebrated reunion with Pink Floyd at Abbey Road during the 1975 sessions for the 'Wish You Were Here' album. Those close to the Floyd believed the band were dangerously close to splitting up. Worn out by an endless series of tours and recording sessions, their efforts to produce a successor to the phenomenally successful 'Dark Side Of The Moon' album were becoming increasingly tortuous. Gilmour insists that the album itself was not dedicated to Barrett but its opening track and key song 'Shine On You Crazy Diamond' is clearly a thinly-veiled tribute. It was developed from the mournful guitar motif played by Gilmour at the start of the 26-minute piece. Gilmour: "I found it by accident but it stirred something in me and I kept playing it. It obviously worked because Roger said: 'Hey, what's that you're playing?'"

Midway through the album, the band heard a strange rumour that Syd had been spotted outside Harrods wearing a large Yogi Bear necktie. They didn't pay much attention as such Barrett tales were by now commonplace. They were therefore quite unprepared for the events of June 5 when Gilmour noticed a shaven-headed, overweight figure walking rather absent-mindedly around Studio Three at Abbey Road: "This guy was walking around looking at the equipment and at first I didn't take much notice because I thought it was one of EMI's staff boffins. Then later he came into the control room. He was there for a long time and we were all whispering: 'Who the fuck's this funny geezer?' I think I was the first to recognise him."

Storm Thorgeson, who arrived for Gilmour's wedding reception later that same day, recalls Syd wearing a white mackintosh with white shoes and carrying a white bag. "Two or three people cried. He sat round and talked for a bit but he wasn't really there."

Andrew King, one of the invited wedding guests, thought Barrett looked like "the type of bloke who serves you in a hamburger bar in Kansas City." He adds: "He was fat and his hair was thinning on top. He was wearing a very short-sleeved sports shirt and American-type slacks. The Floyd took it very badly. What could they say? But everyone else had their problems and they knew Syd still had a good income."

Jerry Shirley was equally shocked when he attended the wedding banquet in the EMI canteen that afternoon: "Sitting opposite me was this hulk with a bald head. He must have weighed about 15 stone. While I was eating this guy was looking at me rather strangely and smiling. I thought he was a Hare Krishna freak until Dave, who was sitting a few places down on the other side, saw I was unnerved and motioned me over. I went round and he said: 'Do you know who that is?' Just as he said that I was looking at the guy from the side and something about his profile made me realise it was Syd. I went over and asked him how things were going. He was chuckling over the fact that I hadn't recognised him. Syd spent the rest of the meal looking at my wife in a disconcerting manner and I think he disappeared as mysteriously as he had arrived."

None of the Floyd have seen Syd from that day to this, but a month later their headlining festival appearance in the grounds of the stately home at Knebworth, Hertfordshire, was the setting for another strange incident. The band's first set was a complete rendition of the songs on 'Wish You Were Here'. Roy Harper sang on 'Have A Cigar' just as he did on the album version. According to Harper, who was also managed by Blackhill, a set of photographs were taken earlier in the day when a Floyd-versus-Blackhill cricket match was held in the festival grounds.

Harper: "When the snaps were passed round at Abbey Road a week later, somebody said: 'My God, that's Syd!' We all crowded round to have a look and I'm absolutely certain it was Syd. There was this bald overweight figure actually standing next to me in one of the photos yet no one could remember seeing him there at the time."

The tale is brusquely dismissed by Gilmour as: "Just another of those stupid stories. The idea of Syd being this spectre hanging over us is complete shit." Even so, the story comes from a number of different sources and Syd wouldn't have found it that difficult to reach Knebworth from London. Considering his physical appearance, the fact no one recognised him is not too surprising. He was the subject of at least one of the songs in the Floyd's set so it would be natural for him to want to see its first public performance. When Rogers Waters had played 'Shine On' to him at Abbey Road, Syd had reportedly said it sounded "a bit old."

Waters explained how the song evolved: "It was very strange. I don't know why I started writing those lyrics about Syd. I think because that phrase of Dave's was an extremely mournful kind of sound, but it was a long time before the 'Wish You Were Here' recording sessions when Syd's state could be seen as symbolic of the general state of the group, that is very fragmented.

"I'm very sad about Syd. Of course he was important and the band would never have fucking started without him because he was writing all the material. It couldn't have happened without him but on the other hand it couldn't have gone on with him. 'Shine On' is not really about Syd – he's just a symbol for all the extremes of absence some people have to indulge in because it's the only way they can cope with how fucking sad it is, modern life, to withdraw completely. I found that terribly sad."

1976 is remembered as the year of the punk rock explosion and the overthrow of traditional heroes and values. A decade after the apogee of Swinging London, it was regarded as a sin to profess a liking for The Beatles or The Stones – a crime that Malcolm McLaren used as an excuse to sack Glen Matlock from The Sex Pistols. Although Johnny Rotten strutted down the Kings Road in an 'I hate Pink Floyd' T-shirt, Syd himself was far from an object of derision.

Early that year, The Pistols' art director Jamie Reid contacted Barrett expert Bernard White about the possibility of Syd producing the group's first album. The Pistols' Machiavellian manager Malcolm McLaren was a big Barrett fan. White, of course, was unable to contact Syd, still resolutely locked away in his high-class fortress, and The Pistols were similarly unsuccessful during a brief but tumultuous stay at Chelsea Cloisters. When the band's infamy is taken into account, Syd's reluctance to open his door to McLaren's spiky-haired mob is perhaps not surprising.

While Syd proved an elusive quarry for The Pistols, he developed a habit of haunting old friends and acquaintances when least expected. Producer Malcolm Jones met Barrett outside the HMV store and Jack Monck exchanged a brief greeting with him in Charing Cross Road. On a trip to Harrods, Twink was standing on the up escalator and was startled to see Barrett pass by silently on the one going down. On another occasion, Syd burst into Jenner and King's Blackhill office in Bayswater as if such an appearance warranted not a hint of surprise. Although they were no longer handling his affairs, Syd asked for, and was given, his passport. No one asked, or was told, why he wanted it.

Syd's heavyweight look made these occasional sightings all the more shocking. No one could quite believe how the once-skeletal Barrett frame had transformed so dramatically in such a short space of time.

Capital Radio DJ Nicky Horne attempted to interview Syd and later told *The News Of The World:* "I knocked on the door and this huge fat man answered wearing only pyjama trousers. He'd shaved off his eyebrows and looked incredibly strange. I thought he was a minder. He looked down at me and said 'Syd can't talk.' When I told Dave Gilmour he said the man had been Syd and he'd been telling the truth. He really couldn't talk any more."

Bernard White: "When I saw a photo of Syd taken at the 'Wish You Were Here' sessions I just had to sit down. I'd bumped into him only nine months before that and the change was unbelievable."

Syd's growing fondness for Guinness, coupled with boredom and a royalties income that enabled him to dine out at the more expensive London restaurants, were the chief causes of his expanding waistline.

In the summer of 1977, ex-fiancée Gayla Pinion was shopping in South Kensington when she turned and saw Syd: "He stood there juggling a tin of Campbell's soup in one hand and just laughing at me. He must have been a good stone heavier and his hair was cut in a short back and sides." Syd's appearance reminded Gayla of his far-fetched idea of pursuing a medical career. "Standing there in his white shirt and pin-striped suit, he looked just like a doctor." Slightly unnerved and unable to believe this was the man she had nearly married, Gayla prepared to leave the store: "When we got outside I couldn't resist any longer and called after him. He swung round and just said, 'Fancy seeing you here'."

Gayla was surprised when Syd invited her to a pub as he had never drunk much when she was with him. Over a half-pint of cider and the inevitable pint of Guinness, he invited her back to Chelsea Cloisters and a cautious Gayla accepted the offer. "When we got there I found all the curtains were drawn, no windows were open and there was this horrible smell. In the middle of the room was a huge television set." It brought back too many painful memories and declining a cup of tea, Gayla nipped out of the door while Syd pottered about in the kitchen.

The following spring, New York freelance writer Kris DiLorenzo produced an article for *Trouser Press* magazine, undoubtedly the best since Nick Kent's thoughtful study in 1974. Jerry Shirley expressed doubts over whether Syd would ever record again – "He would have to return to this planet long enough for someone to believe that he's got it in him to actually get to the sessions" – and Bryan Morrison cleared up a few mysteries: "He doesn't have any involvement with anything or anybody. He is a recluse with about 25 guitars around him. I see him very rarely. I mean, I know where he is, but he doesn't want to be bothered; he just sits there on his own watching television all day and getting fat. That's what he does."

Asked whether anyone could talk Syd into recording again, Morrison's negative response merely confirmed Shirley's gloomy forecast: "No, it's impossible."

Barrett was firmly anchored in his shell but this did nothing to deter pioneering punk band The Damned from attempting to persuade Syd to produce their second album later that year. Captain Sensible and the rest of the band were Barrett freaks who hoped the Madcap's presence would give the album an eccentric slant and early Floyd influence. Captain Sensible: "During rehearsals we discovered we all loved the early Floyd stuff so we approached some people who knew Syd but they said it wasn't really on. In the end we had to make do with Nick Mason and he didn't have a clue." In her biography *The Book Of The Damned* Carol Clerk described 'Music For Pleasure' as a "dismal desperate record" and quoted the band saying Mason was not the man for the job. "He just didn't know the band, didn't understand the energy that we had before. Also the songs weren't really there and he didn't give us any guidance in that. We were trying to get into his world and he was trying to get into ours and the two never met. There was a hell of a lot of disillusionment."

Floyd had long since come to accept that even a decade after the split they would never be free of Barrett's influence. Questions on Barrett were an obligatory part of every interview. Rick Wright was quizzed about his former colleague in an interview on Montreal Radio's *The Pringle Show* in December 1978. "He (Syd) is probably like he has been for the past seven years. He's very weird. I haven't seen him for years. The last time I saw him was when we did 'Wish You Were Here' and he just turned up. I don't know what he's like in his head because he does not talk at all. It's very sad. He can't relate to anyone. He's not a vegetable; his brain's ticking away, but just somewhere else completely. He literally is on another planet."

Wright was asked whether he thought drugs had contributed to Syd's decline: "The drugs don't cause these things. Drugs are just a catalyst if you like. It has to be in your brain first of all – for example, some people can take acid every day of their life and come out of it all right. I know he took the whole lot at this period of time but if he hadn't taken it, I still think he would have gone the way he has; that's the thing. But you never know. You can't tell. (Syd) did get more and more into a group of people who were acidheads which we tried to stop because we could see it was going to destroy him. They won and we lost, I'm afraid."

Roger Waters, who felt Barrett's influence on the latter-day Floyd was grossly exaggerated, was driven to exasperation by the incessant probing of interviewers. In a 1976 interview with

Street Life, which first appeared in the French monthly *Rock Et Folk*, he was reminded that he had recently described Syd as "slobbish, empty and incapable of creativity."

Waters: "Really? My violent reaction is explained by getting snowed under with gossips and snippets that each and everybody put out about Syd. These wouldn't have been brought up if Syd had had some success. Or if we hadn't had any ourselves. For my part I've never read an intelligent piece about Syd Barrett in any magazine. Never. No one knows what they are talking about. Only us, the people who knew him and who still know him a bit. Only we know the facts, how he lived, what happened to him, why he was doing certain things. They make me laugh all these journalists and their rubbish. In actual fact I wrote that song 'Shine On' above all to see the reactions of those people who reckon they know and understand Syd Barrett. There's a feeling in that piece, I don't know, that sort of indefinable, inevitable melancholy about the disappearance of Syd . . . because he's left, withdrawn so far away that, as far as we're concerned, he's no longer there."

The years of frivolous spending were coming to an end for Barrett. What had once seemed a bottomless pit of royalties ran dry and rising rents made it impossible for him to stay at Chelsea Cloisters. The following year, 1979, saw him back with his mother in Cambridge – a declared bankrupt.

Syd's return home coincided with a great wave of publicity for the release of Pink Floyd's album 'The Wall'. Floyd took 'Another Brick In The Wall' to the top of the singles charts and there was speculation that Syd had inspired some of Waters' surreal visions. When a New York DJ played the record backwards he located a secret message that many believed was a reference to Syd. "Congratulations," it began. "You have just discovered the secret message. Please send your answer to The Old Pink, care of The Funny Farm, Chalfont." Pink Floyd had no comment and it is more than likely that the message was added by some mischievous studio engineer or record pressing plant employee.

But as the subsequent film version of 'The Wall' showed, there was an indisputable element of the Barrett saga in the story of the hero Pink, played by Bob Geldof, whose rise to stardom is accompanied by a descent into madness.

Gilmour: "The central character is based on all sorts of people. Syd was convenient for some of the stories. There was, for example, a swimming pool incident in Los Angeles. Syd fell in, took off his Granny Takes A Trip clothes, and left them lying by the poolside for three days." In the film Geldof cuts himself and, lying prostrate in a hotel pool, turns the water blood-red.

The album was an extraordinary commercial success. EMI shipped 600,000 sets in four weeks in the UK alone where it was retailing at £8.45 a copy. By the end of January, the figure was over 1,200,000 copies.

The gulf between Syd and his former band could scarcely have been wider. While the Floyd premièred 'The Wall' at the Los Angeles Sports Arena, complete with inflatable pig, an animated film and crashing aeroplane, Barrett was once again ensconced in Cambridge, quietly living with his mother in another part of the city. Apart from a rumour that he turned up at the Abbey Road studio, guitar in hand and intent on resuming his recording career, only to be turned away when no one recognised him, little was heard of the Madcap in 1980.

The following year, a crop of new bands emerged whose image and songwriting was based on sixties psychedelia. Many cited Barrett as a major influence including The Television Personalities whose leader Dan Treacey penned a charming little song to someone he (wrongly) felt was in danger of becoming a forgotten hero. 'I Know Where Syd Barrett Lives' sold several thousand copies, made the independent charts, and was even released in Japan under the misprinted title: 'I Know Where Syd Barrer Lives' – the response of the fanatical Japanese record-buying public is unrecorded.

The band sent a copy of the record – an attempt at copying the Barrett style – to Syd's family who were quite touched. They were not so pleased with some of the dubious publicity the record brought in its wake. First off the mark was *The Sun* newspaper which told its credulous readers that a grotesquely overweight Syd was living in the attic of his mother's home and had taken advantage of one of his mother's shopping trips to nip downstairs and paint the fridge green before returning to his hiding place. Another man claimed to have met a vaguely familiar character enjoying a pint of Guinness in the King's Arms pub in Cambridge. When questioned about the superstar

group he created, he replied: "Pink Floyd? I know the name . . .
I think they owe me some money."

The stories were typical of the questionable Barrett tales that
surfaced that summer. The 'green fridge' episode is the stuff of
which myths are made – an example of how wild rumour can
come to be regarded as fact – and it has been faithfully recycled
over the years, usually when one of the music papers puts out a
'10 Rock Fruitcakes Of Our Time' list. With the passage of time it
has become as much a part of Barrett folklore as the mandrax
incident of 1967.

Reality was far more mundane. Syd's health left a lot to be
desired. He had spent some time in a sanatorium in Essex but
despite the undeniable benefits to his well-being, within weeks
of returning home he was back in hospital to have a stomach
ulcer removed. Feeling stronger by the summer of 1982 and
having amassed a sizeable sum in royalty back-payments, he
once again took up residence at Chelsea Cloisters. His return
was a pleasant surprise for porter Ronnie Salmon in more ways
than one. The prospect of a healthy income from tips and
handouts was restored but he was also amazed at the transfor-
mation in his former benefactor's appearance: "When he left
here, he was as fat as a barrel and his head was shaved. Now
here he was again – the original Syd Barrett looking just like he
had in 1974. His hair had grown long and he was very thin. I
said: 'Christ, you've lost a lot of weight' and he said he'd had a
stomach ulcer."

The expected freebie bonanza never materialised: "He stayed
here for a few weeks and then went back to Cambridge without
even saying goodbye. We haven't seen him since."

Chapter Ten

Unforgotten Hero

U nknown to Barrett, a couple of French journalists were hot on his trail. They spent a week searching the capital for him without success. When they finally traced him to Chelsea Cloisters, our heroes were dismayed to discover he had left a month earlier. Undeterred, they persuaded the estate agent to hand over a bag of Syd's grubby washing and volunteered to return it. Their plan was, to say the least, ingenious. Barrett had diligently avoided all interviews since 1971. Now they had the perfect excuse to meet him.

Arriving in Cambridge, they launched into the final stage of the great Barrett hunt. Things did not go according to plan. For a start, Syd and his mother had moved to another part of the city and their quarry refused to co-operate by taking one of his regular sojourns onto the streets. Amid rising consternation, the French sleuths tracked him down but faced with meeting "the visionary of rock" their nerve failed. Uncertain of the reception that awaited them, they proceeded to hang around Syd's street for a couple of days with cameras at the ready.

This proved an exercise in futility – all they managed to do was annoy the neighbours who naturally objected to a couple of suspicious-looking strangers lurking furtively outside their homes. Eventually one of the men plucked up enough courage to ring the Barrett's doorbell while his photographer companion waited breathlessly in anticipation. The farce that followed was described in the French magazine *Actuel:*

"A shadow looms up at the end of the corridor and comes slowly to meet me.

'Hello.'

We're both surprised at the meeting, our voices tremble slightly.

'I've brought back your laundry.'

SB: 'Oh yes! From Chelsea! Yes . . .'

He's an old, tired man. Very short hair, balding at the temples, drawn features, glassy-eyed with arms hanging at his sides. He's thin with opaque skin.

'I've been trying to see you; I went to Chelsea. They told me there was some washing and that you lived with your mother.'

SB: 'Thanks very much. Do you want some money? Did they make you pay?'

'No really, it's all right. What do you do now? Do you paint?'

SB: 'No, I've just had an op but it's nothing serious. I'm trying to get back (to London) but there's a train strike at the moment.'

'What do you do in your London flat? Do you play your guitar?'

SB: 'No, I watch TV, that's all.'

'Don't you want to play any more?'

SB: 'No, not really. I'll have to find myself a new flat there. But it's difficult. I'll have to wait.'

Now and again he looks at his washing, he fidgets, he smiles.

SB: 'I didn't think I'd get these things back. And I knew I couldn't write for them. I didn't get round to deciding to go back for them. Mum told me she'd ring the office. Thanks all the same.'

He kept trying to finish the conversation. He kept looking out to the garden, to his mother.

'Do you remember Duggie?'

SB: 'Mmm yes . . . I haven't seen him since . . . I haven't been to see anyone in London.'

'All your friends say hello.'

SB: 'Oh, thanks . . . that's nice.'

'Can I take a photo of you?'

SB: 'Yes, of course.'

He smiles, stands to attention and smartens his collar.

'Good, that's it now, thanks.'

He looks at the tree outside his house. I don't know what else to say.

'That tree's lovely.'

SB: 'Yes, but not now . . . they cut it down not long ago . . . before, I really liked it.'

At the back of the house his mum speaks: 'Roger, come and have a cup of tea and say hello to my friends.'

Roger turns towards me, panicked.

SB : ' Mmm good. OK, perhaps we'll see each other in London . . . Bye.'

'Yes, see you soon . . . Bye.'

On leaving, I feel incredibly empty. That's it. Finished.''

Those close to Syd believe the French interview to be genuine as it includes tell-tale phrases that only Barrett would use. The anticlimax the author speaks of is a typical reaction when a fanatical Barrett buff meets ''rock's big visionary'' as the French magazine called him. Fans who feel compelled to seek out their idol come to see Syd Barrett, not the reclusive Roger. The reality brings disillusionment.

When Luca Ferrari, of the Italian Barrett fanzine *Dark Globe*, met Syd he was apparently so disheartened that he immediately wound up the publication. ''It's been a real shock to me because he wasn't very together and his talking was confused,'' said a dismayed Ferrari. ''His hair was so cut . . . he had a very long beard on his face.''

In an interview with *Musician* magazine in December 1982, Dave Gilmour was asked for his opinion on the more extreme Barrett fans: ''It's sad that these people think he's such a wonderful subject, that he's a living legend. He's got uncontrollable things in him that he can't deal with and people think it's a marvellous, wonderful, romantic thing. It's just a sad, sad thing; a very nice and talented person who's just disintegrated. Syd's story is a sad story romanticised by people who don't know anything about it. They've made it fashionable but it's just not that way.''

The never-ending search for Syd has its comical aspects. Mr Sid Barrett, an elderly fenland farmer living near Downham Market, 40 miles North-East of Cambridge, has been the bewildered recipient of countless Barrett inquiries. His wife Pat told the authors in 1990: ''This has been going on for years. We've had loads of letters as well as phone calls from Italy, America and Norway. It's a heck of a job trying to convince these people that they've got the wrong chap. One Italian bloke cut up a bit rough when I told him my Sid was a farmer, and only last week a DJ from Nottingham wrote asking if he could send some tapes. It's quite funny really because my Sid is 72 so he's a bit long in the tooth to be a rock star. He played a bit of piano as a kid and he sings in the bath but that's about it."

The persistence of such Barrett hunters drove the real Syd into an increasingly solitary, totally anonymous existence by the early eighties. His family noticed that he was becoming steadily more reclusive, confining his travels to the local shops. The Cambridge Folk Festival site was nearby and the Barretts were used to curious fans turning up on their doorstep. Syd had occasionally let some in and even shown them around the house, but now he preferred his own company and often refused even to answer the front door. His increasingly frail mother moved out to be looked after by relatives, deepening Syd's isolation. He no longer had a telephone having personally disconnected it.

Rolling Stone magazine tracked down Barrett's Cambridge basement flat and described him as living "like a character from one of his own songs." Libby Gausden felt the same when she bumped into Syd in a supermarket in 1985. "I told him he was still a hero in the outside world and that he ought to go back out there. I couldn't help thinking that he would have written about himself years ago. He would have laughed at the little shopping bag he carried on the handlebars of his bike."

Joe Boyd numbered 'Bike' among "the greatest tracks of all time." Here was Syd using a bike, uncannily similar to the one he describes in the song, to transport himself around his increasingly small world. As they chatted Libby recalled how, even as a teenager, Syd had been fascinated by the solitary English eccentrics he occasionally came across in Cambridge. 'Arnold Layne' was typical of these – a song about a slightly creepy but ultimately harmless oddball written from a sympathetic viewpoint. Syd may not have had Arnold's penchant for stealing women's underwear, but his reclusive lifestyle made Libby think automatically of Barrett's most famous character: "When I told him that he had become Arnold Layne he threw his head back and roared with laughter as if it was the funniest thing he'd ever heard. He thought the whole idea was hilarious."

The mid-eighties were lean years for accurate news of Barrett but it was a period of unparalleled publicity and prosperity for

Pink Floyd. The band's public and highly acrimonious break-up was triggered by the release of 'The Final Cut' in March 1983. Rick Wright had fallen out with Roger Waters after 'The Wall' (on which he received no credit whatsoever) and left – the first personnel change since Gilmour replaced Barrett in 1968 – and the other Floyd members had little involvement in 'The Final Cut' which was essentially a Waters solo album.

The following year saw all the Floyd members embark on solo projects. Dave Gilmour released 'About Face' to generally enthusiastic reviews. Rick Wright teamed up with Dave Harris, formerly of Fashion, to form a short-lived and disappointing outfit called Zee; Roger Waters brought out the marginally more successful 'The Pros And Cons Of Hitch-Hiking', complete with controversial 'sexist' cover, and Nick Mason co-produced his own 'Profiles' album with former 10cc cohort Rick Fenn.

In April, Dave Gilmour, who had toured Europe promoting his new album, played at London's Hammersmith Odeon with The Television Personalities supporting. For reasons best known to themselves, The Personalities followed an unscheduled rendition of 'See Emily Play' by reading out Syd's home address while Gilmour sat fuming in the wings. They were replaced for the subsequent two nights by Billy Bragg, whose manager is Pete Jenner.

In November 1986, Gilmour and Mason confounded the widely-held view that Pink Floyd were finished by issuing a statement saying: "Although Roger Waters quit in December 1985, the group had no intention of disbanding. On the contrary, David Gilmour and Nick Mason, with Rick Wright and producer Bob Ezrin, are currently recording a new album."

Waters launched a swift and angry response saying Pink Floyd was "a spent force creatively." He then began legal proceedings. Through the courts, he made several unsuccessful attempts to prevent the others using the Floyd name saying: "In the best of all possible worlds, my public, the Pink Floyd public, will turn round and say: 'No, this is not Pink Floyd, it meant more than this. No, it shouldn't be just a kind of franchise'."

Waters was in for a shock if he thought the resurrected Floyd could not survive without him. After releasing 'A Momentary Lapse of Reason' in 1987, the three-man Floyd – augmented by percussionist Gary Wallis, second keyboard-player Jon Carin, guitarist Tim Renwick, bass-player Guy Pratt, Scott Page on saxophones, and three-piece female backing vocals – embarked on a world tour which according to the American *Forbes* financial magazine grossed 67 million dollars in one year alone. The tour, a further demonstration of extravagant special effects, showed that the Floyd were still one of the biggest attractions on the stadium circuit. Waters' concurrent solo tour – which show-cased similar highlights from the Floyd songbook – was nowhere near as successful.

If he was at all aware of the public squabbles between Waters and Gilmour in particular, the irony cannot have been lost on the reclusive character who had created the monster in the first place. Barrett's thoughts are unknown as he never discussed Pink Floyd, even when questioned by members of his family. The memory is still there, however, along with a slight feeling of bitterness. Long after he had broken all links with the Floyd, Syd still referred to them as "my band."

In January 1988, EMI brought out the Barrett solo albums on compact disc. *Q* magazine wrote: "He (Syd Barrett) had a natural gift for inventing simple melodies and a nicely disingenuous way of singing them, both of which talents are reduced to self-parody by the childish doodly strums of 'The Madcap Laughs' his first album in 1969. His second and last, 'Barrett', was a more attractive and disciplined effort, but by then the discipline clearly wasn't Syd's thing at all. And by today's standards it still sounds too scrappy to warrant enshrining in CD."

This view was contradicted by the owner of a Swindon record shop a couple of weeks later when Syd's 1970 John Peel radio session was issued on the Strange Fruit label. The *Swindon Evening Advertiser* reported: "Welcome back Syd Barrett – new hero of the compact disc age. Syd's CDs are selling like hot cakes in Swindon. A five-track Syd Barrett CD single is disappearing from the shelves of the town's only CD shop as fast as they can get them in. Owner of the Victoria Road shop, Geoff Miles, says: 'I'm into my third batch of Syd Barrett singles. Who'd believe old Syd would sell so many discs?' The CD comes from a John Peel session of eons ago and comprises the tracks, 'Terrapin', 'Gigolo Aunt', 'Baby Lemonade', 'Two Of A Kind' and 'Effervescent Elephant'. Says Geoff: 'People come into the shop and expect to hear the latest disco music blaring out and they hear Syd Barrett'."

A new rock magazine called *Strange Things* devoted a large part of its first issue to 'The Making Of The Madcap Laughs' – an edited version of Malcolm Jones's booklet published in 1982 – and the April 1988 edition of *Q* carried a comprehensive review of Floyd's entire back catalogue, now available on CD, describing Barrett as "an unbalanced and uniquely gifted writer whose talent turned supernova when he first set foot in a recording studio."

The same month *Record Collector* published an article by Mark Paytress which examined Barrett's career in detail and speculated on the possible release of a rarities album. It was well known that several unreleased Barrett tracks were languishing in EMI's vaults and at least two items had appeared on the bootleg market to confirm the existence of more worthy material. The first of these, the 'Vinyl Sessions' EP, boasted an alternative version of 'Dark Globe', much slower than the issued take, plus the previously unreleased 'Birdy Hop', 'Milky Way' and 'The Word Song'.

These three out-takes from the 'Barrett' album also appeared on another unofficial release, 'El Syd'. Paytress lamented EMI's indecision and said the ball was now firmly in the record company's court. He added: "It is too painfully evident that the adult world appeared too gruesome and altogether unreal for Syd Barrett. Thankfully, he has left behind a fascinating legacy of recordings, almost all of which betray a yearning for the simplicities of childhood, a world inhabited by sequined fans, hopping birds and feathery tongs."

EMI had, over the years, grown accustomed to phone calls, letters and petitions from Barrett fans urging the release of any material remaining in the vaults. Like so much about him, the so-called 'lost' Barrett album had taken on mythical proportions, second-only to a Beatles reunion. By 1988, the clamour was so great that EMI could ignore it no longer. The result in October that year was 'Opel' – a compilation of leftover tracks from the two solo albums. The compilers were honest enough to point out that it was not the lost third album and much of the material had been available on badly mastered bootlegs for some time. Nevertheless, the inclusion of the classic title track and the fact

that Syd's words and music had never before been heard in such
clarity, met with all round approval.

The record was reviewed by Edwin Pouncey in the October 29
edition of *Sounds*: "There is also the bonus of two finds that I've
never seen bootlegged, 'Dolly Rocker' and 'Lanky (Part One)'.
Both prove to be no cheap filler job either, this is classic Syd
Barrett. The curious initiate into Barrett's world would be well
advised to try the official albums before venturing into these
deep, dark waters. For those well-versed in the lore according to
Syd . . . Dive in!"

Q magazine commented: "'Opel' is not the kind of record that
lays the legend to rest, but instead encourages further lamenting
of that legend's premature passing."

Radio One DJ Nicky Campbell was one of the few to give
airtime to 'Opel'. The following interview appeared on his late
night show on October 27.

NC: "On the line from Cambridge, I have Paul Breen. Paul,
thank you very much for taking the time to join us this evening.
In what way are you actually related to Syd Barrett?"

PB: "Syd is my brother-in-law, my wife's brother in fact."

NC: "So you're married to Syd's sister?"

PB: "Yes."

NC: "Logically enough! A lot of people are interested. What is
Syd doing now?"

PB: "Well, he is living in Cambridge and, contrary to public
opinion, he's not living in a field in a barrel somewhere. He is
living in a semi-detached house in a suburb of Cambridge city."

NC: "And he'd be what – 43-years-old?"

PB: "He's 43 or 44. I'm not quite sure at the moment – around
that age."

NC: "You could describe him as a recluse, couldn't you?"

PB: "I think the word 'recluse' is probably emotive. It would
probably be truer to say that he enjoys his own company now
rather than that of others."

NC: "It's a long time since he played any music, does he still
have a guitar or practise music or write music?"

PB: "No, he doesn't play any musical instruments any more.
He's not interested in writing music. He concentrates his
energies these days. He's started to develop an interest, yet
again, in painting, which was originally his main interest back in
the early sixties."

NC: "Of course, because he came from an art school background didn't he?"

PB: "That's right, yes."

NC: "And are lots of the family still alive, apart from yourself?"

PB: "Yes. He's got two brothers and two sisters and his mother's still living in Cambridge. He leads a very normal life. He probably sees her about twice a week; meets her in town and does a bit of shopping with her – you know, a very very ordinary sort of lifestyle."

NC: "Does he ever get recognised?"

PB: "Rarely, I think because since he was a significant public figure, of course, he's aged 20 years and the hair has receded a little. He would be recognisable to someone who knew him 20 years ago, but probably not to people who had just seen him on the album covers or on TV back in the heyday of *Top Of The Pops* and things."

NC: "Does he have any contact at all with the other members of Pink Floyd?"

PB: "Not to my knowledge, no."

NC: "And how does Syd himself view the sixties and his part in it and the whole thing?"

PB: "I think it's part of his life which he prefers to forget now. He had some bad experiences and, thankfully, has come through all the worst of these and is able – fortunately – to lead a normal life in Cambridge."

NC: "So – it's a difficult one to answer, this, but one I'm sure a lot of people would be interested in knowing the answer to – is Syd happy?"

PB: "Yes. Yes, he is. There's a level of contentment now which he probably hasn't felt since before he got involved in music, in fact. He is developing new interests and particularly his painting – which has progressed as the years go by."

NC: "Well, I know he doesn't speak to the press and I don't blame him for that but when you see him Paul pass on our very best wishes to him."

PB: "I will do Nicky."

NC: "And tell him we're still very much enjoying the great music he made."

PB: "OK, I'll tell him so."

Even as this interview was being broadcast, moves that would temporarily shatter Syd's tranquility were underfoot. Its appetite whetted by the many lurid Barrett tales, *The News Of The World* dispatched reporter Mick Hamilton to track him down.

That summer saw the rise in Britain of Acid House, a dance/fashion cult fanned by the media into a mass-market industry. Major labels latched on to the music, High Street stores launched the fashion accessories, newspapers moralised about the drugs. Early Floyd records were among those played at large all-night Acid House parties. Hamilton tried to use Barrett as a symbol of this latest danger to the nation's youth. In September, *The Sun*, sister paper to *The News Of The World*, presented an 'Acid House fashion guide.' Shortly afterwards, in an all too typical mixture of credulity and ignorance, it welcomed the 'groovy and cool' scene with a 'guide to the lingo' and a T-shirt offer. But someone at the paper belatedly realised that 'acid' could refer to LSD and the word 'ecstasy' seen on many Acid House T-shirts was in fact a reference to 'a mind-blowing sex drug' freely available at many of the all-night warehouse parties. By October, *The Sun* had predictably staged a complete about-turn and headlines such as 'Shoot These Evil Acid Barons' and 'Evil Of Ecstasy' had become commonplace on its front page.

Hamilton's double-page spread on Barrett, complete with Acid House 'smiley' logo to justify its existence, appeared at the height of the Acid House backlash. Hamilton told readers that Barrett had trouble stringing a few words together. Barrett's neighbours had become highly protective of him over the years and rarely, if ever, agreed to discuss his situation with curiosity-seekers. Yet Hamilton had the marvellous good fortune to stumble across a neighbour (anonymous of course) who promptly supplied him with a string of juicy quotes. Syd, he said, had been heard inside the house barking like a dog. At other times he shrieked like a lunatic. "God knows what goes on in there. He won't come out for days at a time." Apart from the sensational revelations of this remarkably garrulous 'neighbour', the article included a snatch-photo of Syd dressed "like a dirty tramp" in tatty stained jeans. Judging by Syd's pose in these photographs, it would appear *The News Of The World* photographer pounced just as Barrett was putting out his household rubbish.

Whatever the morality of the situation and the ethical questions involved, publication of the article brought Syd right back into the public eye. *The News Of The World*, whose ranting from the pulpit in 1967 had unwittingly helped launch Barrett on his rocky road to stardom, was still putting the knife in a full 20 years on.

The causes of Syd Barrett's breakdown and gradual withdrawal are many and varied. He is often termed an acid casualty but the real reason is more complex than that. Syd was a rebellious character. From an early age he was extremely attractive and charismatic, but his anarchistic leanings bordered on the obsessional. A clue to his convoluted psyche can be found in a *Disc And Music Echo* profile from 1967. It reveals Barrett's long-held belief in total freedom – he hated to impede or criticise others and despised those who impeded or criticised him. He was fond of saying that all 'middlemen' (record producers, engineers, executives etc) were bad and should be done away with.

When Syd was 16, he discovered The Beatles and was besotted with the idea of becoming a pop star himself. Barrett did not believe in discipline of any kind. What better way of transcending the petty rules of society than by being successful as a pop star with enough wealth to do whatever you pleased? Significantly, it was only after this dream was fulfilled that Syd's real problems emerged. He had yearned to be free of restrictions all his life, yet as a celebrity things were no different and in many ways they were worse. He had money, beautiful girls and colourful clothes but he was expected to live and behave in a certain way – the new set of rules were just as unwelcome. On top of this, Syd's drug-taking, which had always been considerable, grew in proportion to his fame. Just as he was the good-looking member of Pink Floyd who the girls flocked to, so he was also the one showered with gifts of LSD and mandrax. A more stable character might have resisted these pressures but Syd's fragile constitution was well and truly taken over by the rock 'n' roll machine. The death of his father when Syd was 15, and the subsequent free-rein he enjoyed, helped forge his lack of discipline.

If that wasn't enough, Syd was also the musical focus of the group and the man who'd done most to propel them into the big time. As his personal problems multiplied so too did the pressure to produce another hit. Inevitably, the worse his mental condition became, the harder it was to write songs. Many assumed Syd's break with Pink Floyd would mean a fresh start but the damage had already been done. Syd's lyrics are unquestionably at their best on 'Piper At The Gates Of Dawn'. By the time 'The Madcap Laughs' hit the streets two-and-a-half years later, the momentum had been lost. Like many innovators, Barrett discovered he'd been overhauled – and his own quality control was declining.

Pete Jenner: "His real problem is that he's found no way of articulating his creative drive. It's very hard to work on your own; it's very very hard not to have a band where you're bouncing ideas around. If, on top of that, everybody thinks you're a loony, it becomes very difficult indeed."

Andrew King: "I'd always had this feeling that Syd's period would be brief. It's a bit like John Keats if you like. All his poems were written in a very short space of time."

Rick Wright: "If he hadn't had this complete nervous breakdown, he could easily have been one of the greatest songwriters today. I think it's one of the saddest stories in rock 'n' roll, what happened to Syd. He was brilliant – and such a nice guy." (*Musician*, August 1988).

Robyn Hitchcock, former leader of the present-day cult band The Soft Boys, is often compared to Barrett. He puts it another way: "Syd had a very raw and undiluted talent which is probably why it ran out so quickly. What made him, also destroyed him."

It is probably fair to say that if Syd hadn't tampered with the demon acid his recording career would have been longer and it is tempting to believe he might still have been an attraction on the live circuit today. Jenner: "I do feel that the acid had a lot to do with it. Someone with as much imagination, insight and artistic talent as Syd would find it all too hard to handle. Certainly that was the key period when the rot set in as far as I could see. Up to that time, he was no problem – just one of the nicest people."

Pete Townshend: "Syd was someone with psychotic tendencies who by using too much LSD pushed himself over the edge. Remember that LSD was developed for use in psychiatry in clinical circumstances. I only used acid a few times and I found it incredibly disturbing. I have certain psychotic tendencies and found it extremely dangerous for me."

1969 saw the publication of a semi-autobiographical novel called *Groupie* which became something of a *cause célèbre*. Written by Jenny Fabian and Johnny Byrne, it chronicles the confessions of a London groupie. The opening chapter revolves around 'Ben', lead guitarist of the 'Satin Odyssey' who always wears gym shoes as a sort of protest about all the money the group is making. People suggested 'Ben' was directly based on Barrett who the groupie heroine, 'Katie', finds totally removed from the other three members of the group. She also notes that his eyes have "the polished look I'd seen in other people who'd taken too many trips in too short a time."

Katie's interest in Ben soon becomes an obsession and she resolves to 'pull' him when the band play at an Oxford summer ball. Her initial attempt at seduction, in a punt on the river, ends in failure, but when the time comes to leave Katie stows away on board the group's van and manages to entice Ben back to her London flat where he duly becomes another notch on her bed post. Her triumph is short-lived as, soon afterwards, Ben freaks out completely, turning up at a gig with a deathly white face beaded in sweat. He hardly plays a note on stage and Ben's grim colleagues tell Katie "his mind is blown to pieces by all the acid he's dropped."

Katie tells how: "After the first set, Ben said he wanted to get away from the club and sit somewhere quiet. We took a taxi back to my flat, promising to return in time for the second set. He sat down and suddenly started talking about all the people who were putting down the group because they had made it. I told him there would always be people like that but he believed the group had sold out and he couldn't reconcile what he wanted to do with what he was actually doing. Commercialism had nothing to do with being a religious artist, he said.

"I wanted to help, but didn't really understand what was wrong. They were in a position to experiment with new musical ideas and there was nothing Ben couldn't do if he had just half a mind to get it together. I just didn't understand. It was like his mind was burning up right in front of my eyes. This beautiful pop musician, shivering and pouring out his torture and miseries, was something else. He seemed to have lost touch with reality and there's no convincing someone like that. So I kept silent and just listened. When it was time to go he rose without argument and we went back for the second set. This time he made no bones about his problem, nor the effect it was having on him. He went on stage, silent, pale and sweaty again, and just sat on the floor with his guitar in his lap. He stayed like that for the whole set. It was the last time he played for Satin and the last time I saw him. He left for some Spanish monastery to find himself. Satin got themselves a new lead guitarist. They were established and could do without Ben. For me, Satin's magic went with him."

Ben's conflict between being a religious artist and the leader of a big-time pop group is echoed time and again in the reminiscences of those closest to Syd during the winter of 1967/68. Syd's personal crisis, his increasing drug problem and the split with Floyd, coincided with the break-up of his long-term relationship with Lynsey Korner. A combination of circumstances deprived him of her stabilising influence when at his most vulnerable.

Former Cambridge girlfriend Jenny Spires believes Barrett was totally unprepared to deal with the onslaught of fame. He rapidly grew to detest fan worship: "It really confused him. It may sound terribly corny but he always saw himself as an artist and all this Pink Floyd business was something that got terribly out of hand. He never dreamt just how big it would all become. Syd was always consistent in his dealings with people and one thing he really hated was the way fame tended to distance him from others and altered the way certain people viewed him.

"There was a rumour that his drinks were spiked with acid. This may seem hard to believe but he just wasn't the type to go over the top – it would have been someone giving it to him. He wasn't interested in scoring, not even particularly keen on smoking a joint, but these hangers-on encouraged him. That's the terrible irony. The world that wanted him so much, ultimately destroyed him."

Like Ben, Barrett simply went away to find himself. Although absent from the recording scene since 1970, his presence continues to be felt. Marc Almond, of the chart-topping duo Soft Cell, was frequently seen with Syd's solo albums under his arm during his art student days in Leeds and later covered 'Terrapin' as Marc And The Mambas. Julian Cope of The Teardrop Explodes, Robert Smith of The Cure and Dan Treacey of The TV Personalities have all cited Barrett's influence.

Paul Weller of The Jam tried to make his guitar sound like Barrett's for the manic solo on the number one hit 'Start!' and more recently The Jesus And Mary Chain performed Syd's anthem of despair 'Vegetable Man'. Other fans include Siouxsie And The Banshees who declared 'Arnold Layne' a major influence on their third album, and The Clash who at one time wanted Pete Jenner to manage them. Robyn Hitchcock, whose Cambridge background and surreal song-writing led to inevitable comparisons with Barrett, developed something of a phobia about the Madcap. He told *Q* magazine that accusations about his unhealthy Barrett obsession were largely true: "I did let it get out of hand. Syd went beyond being an influence to points where there'd be a takeover. It was quite sinister. It was as if at certain times when I was singing or writing it was no longer me but this other guy. There were times when I thought 'My God, this guy is roosting in my head.' I think I've exorcised that now."

Captain Sensible: "Like the punk thing, Syd was uniquely English and could somehow only have come from Cambridge. When I listen to some of his guitar playing it frightens me."

Barrett is one of the best known rock martyrs but there have been others who, as Nick Kent put it, were "spread out on an altar of acid and sacrificed." Syd's strange story may be unique but parallels can be found in the disintegration of head Beach Boy Brian Wilson, the bizarre solo career of Fleetwood Mac founder Peter Green, and psychedelia pioneer Roky Ericson of The Thirteenth Floor Elevators.

Another cult figure closely compared with Barrett is Arthur Lee, the brilliant but erratic driving force behind influential Los Angeles band Love. Lee was, as we have seen, an early influence on Syd who used the chord sequence from 'My Little Red Book' as the main descending riff in 'Interstellar Overdrive'. Lee disbanded Love in early 1968 claiming the rest of the band "just couldn't cut it." At the press conference to announce Love's demise, producer Bruce Botnick described Lee as "most unusual" and claimed he was on acid 24 hours a day.

Roky Ericson was once described as "America's strongest living parallel to Syd Barrett." Addicted to comic and horror magazines in his youth, he went on to produce 'You're Gonna Miss Me' (on which he was described as sounding like a brain-scrambled Eric Burdon) and songs with titles like 'I Love The Sound Of A Severed Head Bouncing Down The Staircase' and 'Chop Chop Away Lizzie Borden'. Roky spent three years in a mental hospital. He avoided a 10-year prison sentence for possession of marijuana, pleading not guilty on the grounds of insanity.

Problems of a slightly different nature plagued Peter Green who penned early Fleetwood Mac classics such as 'Albatross' and 'Man Of The World' before abandoning the group in early 1970. Green was a man of deep social conscience who apparently couldn't come to terms with the fact that while he was being paid a fortune for playing his guitar, millions were starving to death in Biafra.

Colleagues felt he was never the same after his breakfast was spiked with acid during a tour of Denmark. Whatever the reason, Green drifted away from the music business and worked for some time as a gravedigger. He released a series of increasingly unsuccessful solo albums from 1977 onwards and was still inclined to turn up eight hours late for parties or order several restaurant courses just to see what they looked like. In 1987, a *Sunday Mirror* reporter discovered Green living the life of a vagrant in Richmond. His finger nails were a couple of inches long and his long unkempt hair led to local children referring to him as the wolfman.

The late eighties saw an upsurge of interest in The Only Ones, a seminal punk outfit of a decade earlier whose charismatic leader, Peter Perrett bore an uncanny resemblance to Barrett. Sure enough, when the band split Perrett slipped into obscurity to spark a wealth of bizarre Barrett-like rumours.

None of these musicians has exerted as wide an influence as Barrett. He was, to coin a cliché, simply years ahead of his time. His lyrics were original and inventive and far removed from the standard love and sex themes of the time. He borrowed ideas from the guitar themes of the early sixties but rapidly developed his own distinctive style. He was a superb improviser. The tragedy is that Barrett's recorded work amounts to just three albums and a few loose ends. This limited output is what has kept fans clamouring for more.

His lasting influence was illustrated by the release in May 1987 of 'Beyond The Wildwood – A Tribute To Syd Barrett' on the independent Bam Caruso label. The album featured various 'indie' bands tackling Barrett compositions, with varying degrees of success, and was intended to elaborate on his limited body of work rather than copy it. Alan Duffy, a long-time Barrett fan who compiled the collection, said: "It's the same with any hero who doesn't have a great output – you want more but there isn't any. So I did the next best thing. All the bands wanted to do something for Syd in return for the inspiration he gave them." The record was favourably reviewed and sold over 8,000 copies.

The legend surrounding Barrett continues to grow with every year producing a fresh crop of unlikely but intriguing stories. The south London borough of Southwark was the setting for the most recent report, which arose when environmental health officers from the local council called at a block of flats following a noise complaint. It transpired that local residents were infuriated by loud music emanating from a squat on the top floor. The council officials subsequently confronted a well-spoken man with thinning hair and piercing eyes who lived alone in the squat surrounded by amps and guitars.

The man kept insisting he was "the music business" and had invented rock 'n' roll but "had got left behind." He gave his name as Syd Barrett and invited the officials to listen to some of his songs – an offer they declined. When they called back a few days later the mysterious occupant and his few possessions had vanished.

Pete Townshend: "Syd is a case of someone who showed fantastic promise and could have been a tremendously innovative person and a dynamic electrifying performer but was frustrated either by psychiatric problems or psychosis irritated by drug use."

Nick Kent: "Syd Barrett was simply a brilliant, innovative songwriter whose genius was somehow amputated leaving him hamstrung in a lonely limbo accompanied only by a stunted creativity and a kind of helpless illogical schizophrenia."

Roger Waters, who for years regarded Syd as something of a threat – "because of all the bollocks written about him and us" – remains emotionally involved. He told *The Observer* newspaper on July 12, 1987: "I dreamt about him only last night. It was in the open and he was still gone but I sat down and talked to him and it felt good. He was still saying things I wasn't in a position to understand, but I was supporting him and he was accepting it. We were both happy."

The supreme irony is that a musician of Barrett's unquestioned ability is today mainly remembered for semi-authentic acts of drug-inspired lunacy.

Dave Gilmour: "He was one of these people who really shine, yet no one interested in him now ever saw that side because Syd was 'gone' so quickly."

In 1988, Nick Mason told *Musician* that one of the reasons the Barrett legend had persisted was "the James Dean syndrome, that thing of not fulfilling what seems to be your destiny.

"He seems reasonably content," Mason added, "but he's certainly not able to function really and he can't be put back to work. There's a million people out there who'd love to see Syd do another album, come back and all that. I just think that it's quite beyond him."

Epilogue

Almost 20 years since he last recorded or wrote any music, interest in Syd Barrett's work remains unbelievably high.

In April 1992, a year after the publication of the first edition of this book, the authors received a long distance phone call out of the blue from America. The caller was Tim Sommer, a senior A&R executive at Atlantic Records in Sunset Boulevard, California, who had a remarkable proposition to put to the Barrett family.

The prestigious record label was prepared to pay up to £200,000 for any new Barrett material, no matter how basic the recording might be.

"If desired, these recordings could be made at Syd's home in just a few hours and he need not be involved in any promotion or any other facets of the project whatsoever," said Sommer, who was acting on his own initiative in the certain knowledge that Atlantic would back his idea.

"He need not even be photographed. If acceptable to Syd and his family, his entire involvement could be limited to strumming a few songs in his living room. The songs could be of any nature, could reflect any state of art Syd is capable of achieving – fragmentary, covers, acapella, non-pop, even entirely instrumental or, for that matter, spoken word. I have no expectations other than to make money available to Syd in exchange for new work – any work – on tape."

The offer reflected just how eager the record industry is to cash in on the phenomenal long term interest in any star whose potential has not been fully milked. Yet, for once it was an offer that appeared to be made out of genuine respect for the artist.

Tim Sommer and Atlantic later followed up their initial inquiry with a letter to the Barrett family which they asked the authors to pass on to Syd's sister Rosemary Breen. Here is the full proposal put to her:

"Dear Mrs Breen,

I do understand that fame and the public spotlight has not necessarily been kind to your family, and any intrusion on your privacy, especially when it involves an inquiry about your brother, must be difficult.

As a long-time fan of his music, I must not only respect the work he did during his creatively fruitful years, but also the subsequent life choices that he has made.

First let me introduce myself. I am an executive at Atlantic Records, a major and reputable label with a long and illustrious history. Your brother's music has long been a source of joy and inspiration to me and, due to its often painful honesty and originality, a standard I often turn to to judge other artists.

I would be interested in discussing a logistical and financial package that would make a new recording by Roger Barrett possible. I know this is a difficult and sensitive subject and I have no desire to integrate Roger or your family in any of the machinations of the music business nor infringe on Roger and the family's privacy.

Believe me I have no intention of 'bringing back Syd', merely documenting whatever music and art Roger is capable of making. A recording could be made in your front room, in an afternoon, and that could be the end of Roger's involvement. I do not expect anything remotely pop or commercial. This would be an unconventional project and could take an unconventional form.

For the rights to release a new Roger Barrett recording (as stated, of any nature, excepting, of course, one which would embarrass Roger or reflect badly on him), I would pay you £75,000. This, of course, would be an advance on royalties and other monies this recording would generate, so the potential exists to earn far more than this.

Needless to say, we would assume all recording costs and

if any further involvement on Roger's behalf was involved - say if we were to purchase some of his artwork for an album sleeve - an additional fee could be involved.

I understand that Roger and your family most likely have little interest in the music industry and in capitalising on Roger's fame and legend. But perhaps the right package would appeal to you at this time.

I am willing to come to the UK at any moment to talk about this proposition with you. I am extremely open to discussing any facet of this offer and constructing or amending any portion of this plan. Perhaps what I am willing to offer, a decent amount of money and a guarantee of privacy, dignity and simplicity, has never been offered to you at the right time and in the right shape."

Sommer expanded on the idea in consultation with the authors: "We would be *very* satisfied with a package that included just three or four songs," he said. "Another way of doing it might be to take Roger into a local studio with a group of sympathetic musicians, turn on the tape deck and just see what happened. Off the top of my head, I'd suggest Peter Buck and Mike Mills of REM, and perhaps Robyn Hitchcock, all of whom are good friends of mine and would most certainly do this in the blink of an eye."

It was a bold plan, but also a shrewd one. Even without the involvement of major names such as REM, the first new Syd Barrett songs in nearly a quarter of a century would almost certainly recoup Atlantic's outlay in a matter of weeks.

It was no surprise when the Barrett family passed on the offer. They believe Syd is happier today than at any time since the early days of Pink Floyd. They are convinced that a major factor in that contentment is the fact that he shields himself away from the pressures of the music business and the glare of publicity that he knows only too well inevitably accompanies it.

Nevertheless Syd's fame shows no sign of diminishing and the release of a new (at the time of writing) box set, containing 19 Barrett outtakes, only serves to add to the respect he continues to enjoy. The set, appropriately titled 'Crazy

Diamond – The Complete Syd Barrett', contains his two solo LPs, the collection of previously released rarities, 'Opel', and a number of alternative takes. Brian Hogg's sleeve notes also note that during their research for this set, EMI unearthed a 1974 Barrett session at Abbey Road but none of the material was worth using. For reasons which cannot be explained, this tape was not made available to the compilers when 'Opel' was put together.

"It was just instrumental doodlings," says Hogg of the 1974 tape." Obviously someone had taken Syd into the studio for four or five days in the hope that he would come up with something. A vocal mike was left on, but there's no vocals, just some bluesy chord changes. It's not even a bedroom tape."

The exhaustive sleeve notes and deluxe packaging of 'Crazy Diamond' prompted David Cavanagh to comment in his review for *Select* magazine: "It's good to see the legend being looked after".

Q magazine, meanwhile, added that "it displayed the glorious indiscipline of Syd Barrett to the full" and awarded the collection an "excellent" four-star rating.

Others were less appreciative including *New Musical Express* which labelled the collection "A Syd Casualty" that "underscored his failings" and *Melody Maker* which dismissed the bonus tracks as "literally pathetic".

In general, though, such criticism was aimed more at EMI's decision to release alternative takes that perhaps should best have been left in the vaults, as well as the better known 'Madcap Laughs', 'Barrett' and 'Opel' tracks which Syd's many devoted admirers know and love.

Of far more merit, to the authors' minds at least, would have been a separate release for the "bonus" CD included in the lavish and expensively-packaged 'Shine On' box set which serves as a Pink Floyd career retrospective. Sadly Floyd fans were taken for a ride on the EMI gravy train by being asked to pay over £100 for a collection of eight LPs that every self-respecting follower of the group would undoubtedly already have. To add insult to injury, someone took it upon themselves not to include Syd's masterpiece, the début Floyd LP 'The Piper At The Gates Of Dawn'.

The bait was an enticing 10-track collection of Floyd singles and rarities never before released on CD and sadly thousands of Floyd fans took it, making 'Shine On' one of the best-selling box sets of 1993. The 33-minute gem, titled 'The Early Years' brought together the two singles, 'Arnold Layne' and 'See Emily Play', from which the Barrett "genius" tag really sprang, coupling them with their rare B-sides, the flop third single 'Apples And Oranges' and other early Pink Floyd singles previously unreleased on CD. Together with the legendary, and shamefully still unreleased, Syd-penned 'Vegetable Man' and 'Scream Thy Last Scream', EMI would have a truly worthwhile "new" product that they could have marketed with a vengeance without fear of criticism. Barrett fans can only hope they listen to pleas such as this one and eventually do the job properly.

Some small consolation was offered by what is perhaps the most unusual item of Barrett lore to see the light of day in recent years, the June 1993 release of a two-part 12-minute silent film entitled *Syd Barrett's First Trip* which was, indeed, footage of Syd gorging on magic mushrooms for the first time ever, in the Gog Magog Hills outside Cambridge in 1966. Filmed by Syd's film student friend Nigel Lesmoir-Gordon on standard 8mm film, it has been transferred to video and features scratchy footage of Syd in a quarry playing around with mushrooms, placing them over his eyes and staring up into the sky. The second part of this video was shot outside Abbey Road Studios in April of 1967 and features the four members of Pink Floyd cavorting around just after they'd signed their record deal with EMI.

It is difficult to imagine the commercial attractions of a 12-minute silent film, but few would deny that Syd Barrett's first acid trip was a momentous occasion in the history of rock. As it turned out, it was also a tragedy.

Syd Barrett, or Roger as everyone now calls him, is today the antithesis of the colourful sixties rock star that so many fans remember. A balding, rather heavy set figure who lives alone in his Cambridge flat, he seldom ventures into the centre of town.

His brother-in-law Paul Breen says of his current lifestyle:

"He's improving with age, like good wine, and is happy to get on with his life. He doesn't really see anyone, apart from his sister, and clearly enjoys his own company. He does not really show much emotion but certainly gives the impression that he is comfortably settled into his way of life.

"We obviously gave the Atlantic offer considerable thought but everyone felt that far from improving his position it could actually do a great deal of harm by putting things into his mind that would be confusing to him. As he has at last achieved a degree of contentment in his life, the last thing we would want to do was rock the boat."

The only regular interruptions in Syd's middle-aged tranquillity are the fanatical fans who still turn up on his door hoping to find some spark of the genius they have come to admire - or at least to tell him what his music means to them. If Syd decides to open the door, he finds conversation slightly traumatic and usually thinks of an excuse to bring it to an end as quickly as possible.

"I would say it's still a weekly occurrence," says Paul Breen. "He just tells them he's not interested and shuts the door. For some reason most of them seem to come from northern Scandinavia. I have no idea how they find out where he lives."

In a bid to stem this invasive tide, the following letter appeared in the February 26 edition of *The Guardian* newspaper in 1990, in response to a reader who wanted to know if Syd Barrett was indeed still alive. Syd's elder brother Alan J Barrett wrote: "Any rumour of his death was a gross exaggeration. He is alive and well and living happily in Cambridge. He spends most of his time thinking, writing and painting. He has no further active interest in music and wishes to be left to lead a quiet life."

However, with the Barrett family's permission, the authors paid Syd a visit for the purposes of researching this book.

Although his family had told him that a book was being written about his life, past and present, Syd's instant response was that he would not be able to remember anything about his days with Pink Floyd. But Paul Breen suggested a call at Syd's door might, just might, prompt him to speak of days gone by.

The day in question was FA Cup final day and the Cambridge streets were virtually deserted. Still flouting convention, Syd chose kick-off time to leave his house for the shops - an ideal opportunity to stock up on painting equipment while few people were around to disturb him. Despite forewarning of Syd's condition, it is still a shock to meet him; but he is far from the wild character depicted by *The News Of The World*. There is no howling behind the walls of his semi-detached haven. Instead a knock on the door is met with the nervous shuffling of feet from within. The door swings ajar - no more than a few inches – and the one-time king of Middle Earth peers timidly round the woodwork. He's busy watching the football and no, he doesn't think his thoughts on Pink Floyd or his later music would be of much use. With that he returns to his peace.

So what does Syd do behind the door that so many people are still fascinated enough to try and look around?

Up until a couple of years ago he spent much of his time chain-smoking and watching his beloved television. He still watches *Top Of The Pops* every week and owns a record player, though his record collection these days consists mainly of classical music.

According to Paul Breen: "He does not paint as much as he used to and his recent artwork has been surprisingly traditional, a country cottage, a vase of flowers, nothing of an abstract nature. It is of a very good standard and reveals a tremendous amount of latent talent. There was some talk of putting on an exhibition of his work in Cambridge but it never got off the ground. We would only have considered that if he was desperately short of money and, fortunately, he has a very good income."

As well as invalidity pension that Syd has received ever since his breakdown, his body of recorded work still brings in healthy royalty cheques thanks in part to CD re-releases and new works such as the recent 'Crazy Diamond' box set which included long forgotten alternate versions of many of his solo songs.

"He's comfortably off," says Paul Breen. "It never ceases to amaze me how many royalties still flood in for someone who has not recorded anything in 26 years, or whenever it was."

And Syd has found a new outlet for his creative talents.

"At the moment he is writing *The History of Art* which covers all aspects of the subject," Paul Breen told us. "He has a lot of interesting stuff down on paper and has also input a great deal of it onto his personal computer. He has no desire to have it published because he is not remotely interested in anything commercial. He is simply doing it for entertainment."

So who knows perhaps, the genius that gave the world 'Arnold Layne' and 'See Emily Play' does have more to give should Atlantic Records ever persuade the family to change their minds?

The following is not another Barrett rumour. It is a true story and fans will no doubt read into it what they will.

One day, not long ago, Syd visited Paul Breen, who runs a Cambridge Hotel. Sitting in the hotel office, Syd's attention was drawn to his brother-in-law's guitar lying in a corner of the room. At one point Mr Breen was called away. On his return he found Syd holding the guitar and gently strumming a tune. Realising he'd been caught red-handed, Syd dropped the instrument like a stone and turned away sheepishly . . . The Madcap laughed.

Where Are They Now?

JOHN "TWINK" ALDER was last reported running a record shop in Southend.

WINIFRED BARRETT, Syd's mother, sadly died in September 1991 at the ripe old age of 86. Syd was naturally very upset but apparently took the news quite well.

JOE BOYD is head of the successful Hannibal Records company.

CHRIS "CHIMP" CHAMBERLAIN, Syd's Camberwell art tutor, died of cancer in 1986.

PIP CARTER, Pink Floyd's original lights man and the person closest to Syd during the band's meteoric rise, died after a drunken brawl in Cambridge in October 1988 following a long battle against drug addiction. Dave Gilmour attended his funeral.

CHRIS DENNIS runs a recording studio in Chatteris, near Cambridge.

DUGGIE FIELDS is still well known in avant garde art circles and his name occasionally appears in newspaper art columns. He continues to live in the Earls Court flat he shared with Syd, dealing courteously with occasional Barrett inquiries from fans or journalists.

LIBBY GAUSDEN (CHISMAN) is married to a finance director and lives in London. She has a 19-year-old son and a 17-year-old daughter who used Syd as her subject in a GCSE project. She got an 'A' grade.

DAVE GILMOUR elected to take a Pink Floyd sabbatical after the group headlined the Knebworth charity concert in June 1990, helping to raise over £6 million for handicapped children. Among others, he has worked with Pete Townshend, Paul Young, Propaganda and Roy Harper as well as being involved with the One World One Voice charity project. In spring 1993 he and the remaining two members of Pink Floyd regrouped at Gilmour's Astoria houseboat/studio moored at Henley-on-Thames to begin work on a follow-up to 'A Momentary Lapse Of Reason'. A huge new stage show for an accompanying world tour was also in the early stages of production. He has a new girlfriend, Polly Samson, and is separated from his wife Ginger and their four children. Gilmour is also a pilot for his Intrepid Aviation Company who perform at air shows.

JOHN GORDON, Syd's childhood friend, is a graphic designer living in North London. He also works as a magician.

PETER JENNER remains one of the best-known rock managers whose current artists include Billy Bragg, Andy White, Andy Kershaw, The Disposable Heroes of Hiphoprisy, Robyn Hitchcock and Baaba Maal. Jenner is married and lives in Maida Vale.

MALCOLM JONES, whose faith in Syd's abilities never wavered, died of cirrhosis of the liver at the tragically early age of 43 in February 1990. He lived in Wimbledon and had been working on an autobiography.

ANDREW KING now runs the publishing division of Mute Records. He has managed a wide range of artists over years and now manages Ian Dury. He lives in Twickenham, London.

LYNSEY KORNER is married and lives in London. She has broken all links with Syd and politely refuses any interview requests.

MIKE LEONARD still lives in the original Highgate flat where he was landlord to Pink Floyd.

NICK MASON, who married for the second time in 1990, devotes much of his energies to Bam-boo – a company he formed with his partner Rick Fenn – specialising in commercial and library music and film soundtracks. His other company, Ten Tenths, markets Mason's extensive collection of vintage motor cars to film makers and other potential clients. As ever, Nick spends much of his time on the rally driving circuit and, like Dave Gilmour, is a qualified pilot. At the time of writing, his much–vaunted video history and accompanying book on Pink Floyd showed no signs of an appearance. He lives in Hampstead.

JACK MONCK lives in Hackney where he continues to write and record songs in his home recording studio. In spring 1993 he had a limited edition of 200 cassettes produced which he distributed among record companies and friends.

GEOFF MOTT is a teacher in London.

IAN MOORE (IMO) remains a close Floyd associate, often working as Dave Gilmour's unofficial housekeeper when the latter is away on tour. He has made occasional appearances in videos directed by Storm Thorgeson including Nick Kershaw's 'The Riddle'.

GAYLA PINION is a set dresser for television commercials. She has a young son and divides her time between London and West Germany where her boyfriend lives.

JENNY SPIRES (NOSHAD) is married and lives in Cambridge. She is a housewife.

STORM THORGESON's Hypgnosis company folded in 1983 but he continues to design record sleeves including the Floyd's 'A Momentary Lapse Of Reason' and 'Delicate Sound Of Thunder'. Based in London, he has also worked as a film director on rock videos and commercials. He worked on the promo films and stage backdrop for Floyd's 'Lapse' album and tour, he is collaborating on Nick Mason's book on the history of Pink Floyd and helped create the lavish packaging for EMI's farcical 'Shine On' box set. The record company shows no signs of relenting to the increasing pressure for the "free" bonus CD of early Pink Floyd tracks, including Syd's 'Apples and Oranges', to be released separately.

ROGER WATERS, whose solo career has so far failed to match that of his former group, followed The Wall concert in Berlin in July 1990 with yet another doom-laden LP, 'Amused To Death', which was greeted with the usual dismay by critics. At the time of writing the opera he is said to have written remains in the can. He lives in Richmond, London.

CLIVE WELHAM stays in regular contact with his old mate Dave Gilmour. He works for the Cambridge University Press and still plays drums on the club circuit in a band called Executive Suite.

RICK WRIGHT married his Greek girlfriend and kept a characteristically low profile after Knebworth 90. He spends a large part of his time cruising around the West Indies in his yacht. Rick played with Pink Floyd at the Chelsea Arts Ball at the Royal Albert Hall on October 11, 1992.

Appendix 2

Syd Barrett Discography

Catalogue numbers and label information are given for the most recent UK CD versions of recordings listed, unless otherwise stated.

With Pink Floyd
N.B All titles in this section are Barrett compositions unless marked otherwise.

Arnold Layne/Candy And A Currant Bun (7")
Columbia DB 8156
March 1967

See Emily Play/Scarecrow (7")
Columbia DB 8214
June 1967

THE PIPER AT THE GATES OF DAWN
Astronomy Domine; Lucifer Sam; Matilda Mother; Flaming; Pow R. Toc H. (Barrett, Waters, Wright, Mason); Take Up Thy Stethoscope And Walk (Waters); Interstellar Overdrive (Barrett, Waters, Wright, Mason); The Gnome; Chapter 24; The Scarecrow; Bike.
EMI CDP 7 46384 2
August 1967
Original LP: Columbia SCX 6258. A mono version (SC 6258) featured some substantially different mixes.

THE PIPER AT THE GATES OF DAWN
See Emily Play; Pow R Toc H; Take Up Thy Stethoscope & Walk;

Lucifer Sam; Matilda Mother; The Scarecrow; The Gnome; Chapter 24; Interstellar Overdrive
TOWER ST 5093 (Vinyl Only)
US Version – note different tracklist. Also issued in mono, without the 'S' in the catalogue numbers.

TONITE LETS ALL MAKE LOVE IN LONDON
See For Miles SEE CD 258
1968
Includes **'Interstellar Overdrive'** (full version and two short extracts) and **'Nick's Boogie'**. Only the short extracts were included on the original, 1968 soundtrack LP (Instant INLP 002). Both long numbers are available separately on an EP (SEA CD4). **'Interstellar Overdrive'** erroneously credited to Barrett, **'Nick's Boogie'** credited to Pink Floyd. All versions are mono.

Apples And Oranges/Paintbox
(Wright) (7")
Columbia DB 8310
November 1967

Flaming/The Gnome' (7")
Tower 378
1968
US single with different mix of **'Flaming'**.

A SAUCERFUL OF SECRETS
EMI CDP 7 46383 2
Includes three tracks on which Syd definitely plays: **A Saucerful Of Secrets; Jugband Blues; Remember**

A Day (Wright) plus See Saw (Wright) and Set The Controls For The Heart Of The Sun (Waters). Syd may be on the latter two. He is definitely not on the title track, nor, by his own admission, on Corporal Clegg.
June 1968
Originally Columbia SCX 6258. Again, the mono version (SC 6258) featured different mixes.

RELICS
Music For Pleasure MFP 50 397 (not CD)
Includes Arnold Layne; Interstellar Overdrive; See Emily Play; Remember A Day; Bike.
May 1971
Originally Starline SRS 5071. Available on CD (EMI CDAX 701290) only in Australia, where it was temporarily released, without the band's consent.

A NICE PAIR
Harvest SHDW 403 (Vinyl only)
December 1973
PIPER . . . and SAUCERFUL . . . repackaged as a double album.

MASTERS OF ROCK
Harvest 1 C 054–04 299 (Vinyl only)
Includes Chapter 24; Mathilda Mother (sic); Arnold Layne; Candy And A Currant Bun; The Scarecrow; Apples And Oranges; It Would Be So Nice; Paint Box; See Emily Play.
1974
A European only release, of interest since it includes some of the early singles which have never been re-issued outside the SHINE ON box set.

WORKS
Capitol CDP 7 46478 2
Includes Arnold Layne; Set The Controls For The Heart Of The Sun; See Emily Play.
1983
American only compilation.

A CD FULL OF SECRETS
Westwood One Vol. 10
Includes Candy And A Currant Bun; See Emily Play; Flaming (US single version); Apples And Oranges.
1992
American radio-only promo, useful not only because of its wide availability, but for including all the non-album single sides (except, strangely, 'Arnold Layne'), especially the only CD version of the single mix of 'Flaming'.

SHINE ON (CD only box set)
EMI 7 80557 2
November 1992
Eight CD set, including PIPER . . .; SAUCERFUL . . .; WISH YOU WERE HERE and THE WALL (see below). Also contains a book and a bonus disc which includes both sides of each of Pink Floyd's first three singles.

Syd Barrett Solo Recordings
Octopus + Golden Hair
Harvest HAR 5009 (7")
November 1969
Golden Hair is a poem by James Joyce, set to music by Syd.

THE MADCAP LAUGHS
EMI CDP 7 46607 2
January 1970
Terrapin*; No Good Trying*; Love You*; No Man's Land*; Dark Globe; Here I Go*; Octopus; Golden Hair; Long Gone; She Took A Long Cold Look; Feel; If It's In You; Late Night*.
Produced by David Gilmour and Roger Waters (except *, produced by Malcolm Jones). Originally Harvest SHVL 765.

BARRETT
EMI CDP 46606 2
November 1970
**Baby Lemonade; Love Song;
Dominoes; It Is Obvious; Rats;
Maisie; Gigolo Aunt; Waving My
Arms In The Air; I Never Lied To
You; Wined And Dined;
Wolfpack; Effervescing Elephant.**
Produced by David Gilmour and
Richard Wright. Originally Harvest
SHSP 4007

SYD BARRETT
Harvest SHDW 404 (Vinyl only)
September 1974
MADCAP . . . and **BARRETT** re-
packaged as a double album.

THE PEEL SESSION
Strange Fruit SFPSCD 043
February 1988
**Terrapin; Gigolo Aunt;
Effervescing Elephant; Two Of A
Kind; Baby Lemonade**
Recorded for the BBC Radio 1's *Top
Gear* show of May 18, 1970 (DJ John
Peel), with Jerry Shirley (drums)
and David Gilmour (bass).
Produced by John Walters.
Although credited to Syd, many
fans argue that **Two Of A Kind** is a
Rick Wright composition.

OPEL
EMI CDP 7 91206 2
October 1988
**Opel; Clowns & Jugglers
(Octopus); Rats; Golden Hair;
Dolly Rocker; Word Song; Wined
& Dined; Swan Lee (Silas Lang);
Birdie Hop; Let's Spilt; Lanky
(Part 1); Wouldn't You Miss Me
(Dark Globe); Milky Way; Golden
Hair (Instrumental).**
Various producers. Compilation of
demos, alternate takes and
unreleased material. Released in
1988.

OCTOPUS
CEMA S21 57738 (USA): Cleopatra
CLEO 57712 (Canada)
**Octopus; Swan Lee (Silas Lang);
Baby Lemonade; Late Night;
Wined and Dined; Golden Hair;
Gigolo Aunt; Wolf Pack (sic); It Is
Obvious; Lanky (part 1); No Good
Trying; Clowns and Jugglers
(Octopus); Waiving (sic) My Arms
in the Air; Opel.**
Budget price (and quality – the
booklet manages to refer to Sid
Barrett!) compilation featuring
tracks from the first three albums.
Initial US copies had a purple/
black cloth case with free photo &
badge.

**CRAZY DIAMOND –THE
COMPLETE SYD BARRETT**
EMI CDS 7 81412 2
April 1993
3 CD box set. Includes 24 page
booklet, plus Syd's three albums,
each with extra tracks as lilsted
below. There are no new songs, but
some have slightly-altered titles.
**THE MADCAP LAUGHS +
Octopus** (Takes 1 & 2); **It's No
Good Trying** (Take 5); **Love You**
(Take 1); **Love You** (Take 3); **She
Took A Long Cold Look At Me**
(Take 4); **Golden Hair** (Take 5)
BARRETT + Baby Lemonade
(Take 1); **Waving My Arms In The
Air** (Take 1); **I Never Lied To You**
(Take 1); **Love Song** (Take 1);
Dominoes (Take 1); **Dominoes**
(Take 2); **It Is Obvious** (Take 2)
OPEL + Gigolo Aunt (Take 9); **It Is
Obvious** (Take 3); **It Is Obvious**
(Take 5); **Clowns & Jugglers** (Take
1); **Late Night** (Take 2);
Effervescing Elephant (Take 2)

Various Artists Compilation LPs Featuring Syd
This section excludes many promo-
only compilations.

PICNIC
Harvest SHSS 1/2 (Vinyl only)
Includes **Terrapin** and an
unfinished recording of **Embryo** by
post-Barrett Pink Floyd. As a result
of the latter, the double album was
soon withdrawn.

**HARVEST HERITAGE - 20
GREATS**
Harvest SHSM 2020 (Vinyl only)
Includes **Octopus**.

THE HARVEST STORY VOL. 1
Harvest EG 26 0097 1 (Vinyl only)
Includes **Love You.**

BEFORE THE FALL
Strange Fruit Records SFRCD 203
Includes the BBC session version of
Baby Lemonade.

RCD MAGAZINE
The free compilation CD with Vol 1
No 11 included the original version
of **'Dominoes'**, to promote the
CRAZY DIAMOND box set.

Songs About Syd

Kevin Ayers
BANANAMOUR
BGOCD 142
'Oh! Wot A Dream' is about Syd.

Bond & Brown
**TWO HEADS ARE BETTER
THAN ONE**
See For Miles SEECD 345
The punningly titled track 'Mass
Debate' is described as a "Tribute
to Syd Barrett's **'Arnold Layne'**".

The Chills
SOFT BOMB
Slash 828 322 – 2
'Song for Randy Newman, Etc.'
namechecks Syd.

Five Thirty
'Supernova'
East West 9031 – 74991 – 2
The sleeve of this CD single
included a photograph of Syd,
superimposed onto a picture of a
galaxy. The lyrics are vague, but
may refer to Syd.

Focal Point
'Sycamore Sid'
On **DERAM DAYS**
Decal LIK 9 (Various Artists
Compilation album, vinyl only)
There is debate as to whether this
May 1968 B-side was about Barrett.

Robyn Hitchcock.
**BLACK SNAKE DIAMOND
ROLL**
Aftermath ASTCD1
Includes **'The Man Who Invented
Himself'** – namely Syd.

Marillion
'The Madcap's Embrace'
Unreleased but bootlegged track,
also known as **'Lady Fantasy'.**

Pink Floyd
WISH YOU WERE HERE
EMI CDP 7 46035 2
'Shine On You Crazy Diamond' is
about Syd, other tracks also reflect
his part in the Pink Floyd story.
Also released in Quad and as a
picture disc and coloured vinyl.
'Shine On . . .' also appears on
compilation and live albums.
+
THE WALL
EMI CDP 7 46036 8
Syd is easily recognisable in the
character Pink.

The TV Personalities
**AND DON'T THE KIDS JUST
LOVE IT**
Rough Trade ROUGH 24
Includes **'I Know Where Syd
Barrett Lives'**, previously a single.
Syd appears in the booklet artwork.

Twink
(As Twink and the Fairies)
DO IT '77 EP
Available as "extra tracks" on the
Pink Fairies' **LIVE AT THE
ROUNDHOUSE CD**
Big Beat CDWIK 965
Includes **'Psychadelic Punkeroo'**,
whose title refers to Syd. The song
is credited to "A.Syd."
+
MR. RAINBOW
Twink Records TWK CD1
Includes a re-recording of
'Psychadelic Punkeroo'.

Cover Versions
All About Eve
See Emily Play
Encore during 1993 UK tour.

The Blue Angels
Candy
Solid Records ROC 739 (7")
B-Side is 'Lucifer Sam'.

Alex Bollard Assembly
**Pink Rock - Super Sounds of the
Seventies (sic)**
Star Inc. 86057.
Dutch Pink Floyd 'tribute' album,
includes **'Arnold Layne'** and **'See
Emily Play'**.

The Boomtown Rats
'Arnold Layne'
performed on television in 1982.

David Bowie.
PINUPS
EMI CDP 7 94767 2
Includes **'See Emily Play'**.

Camper Van Beethoven
CAMPER VAN BEETHOVEN
Rough Trade ROUGH 109 (not CD)
Includes **'Interstellar Overdrive'**.

Carnival Art
THRUMDRONE
Situation Two SITU CD 32
Includes **'Octopus'**.

Dean Carter & the High
Commission
'Lucifer Sam'
Performed live.

The Concerned Christians
'See Emily Play'
Details unknown.

The Damned
'Arnold Layne'
Performed live
+
'Lucifer Sam'
Performed on television, plus live
as Naz Momad and the
Nightmares.

The Dolphins
'She Took A Long Cold Look'
Single, 1991, details unknown.

Dr Phibes
THE DARK SIDE OF THE POOL
(Various Artists Compilation
album, vinyl only)
Liquid Noise Records
Includes **'Lucifer Sam'**. Also
performed live.

Eat
'Lucifer Sam'
Performed live.

Eclipse
Brazilian Pink Floyd tribute band
who perform **'Lucifer Sam'**;
'Arnold Layne'; **'Matilda Mother'**;
'See Emily Play' and others.

Engine Alley
'Bike'
Performed on Irish radio, 1991.

Family Fodder
'No Man's Land'
Details unknown.

Faust
'Wined & Dined'
Details unknown.

Fortran 5
Crazy Earth
Mute 113
12" Single includes **'L'Essence De Syd'** mix, with samples from **'The Gnome'**
+
BLUES
Mute CD STUMM 79
Includes two versions of **'Bike'** ('Sid Sings Syd' and 'Steve James Mix'), with the lyrics sampled from Sid James' spoken parts in Bless This House, Hancock's Half Hour and the Carry On films (Steve James is his son). Also includes **Crazy Earth.**

Ghostdance
'See Emily Play'
Performed live (once!).

Graded Grains
'Lucifer Sam'
Details unknown.

The Grapes of Wrath
'See Emily Play'
Performed live.

The Igloos
Wolf
Fresh Records FRESH 23 (7" single)
B-side is 'Octopus'.

Intastella
'Intastella Overdrive' (sic)
Performed live.

Jesus & Mary Chain
Upside Down
Creation CRE 012 (7" single)
B-side is **'Vegetable Man'**.

Knox
'Gigolo Aunt'
Armagedon AS003 (7" single).

La Muerte
BLACK GOD/ WHITE DEVIL
Sex Wax Records SWCD 691017
Belgian release including **'Lucifer Sam'**.

London PX
'Arnold Layne'
Terrapin Records SYD1 (flexi-single).

Love & Rockets
Kundalini Express
Beggars Banquet BEG 163T (12" single)
Extra track on B-side is **'Lucifer Sam'**.

Marc And The Mambas
UNTITLED
Some Bizarre 510 2984
Includes **'Terrapin'**.

Marigolds
'Two Of a Kind'
Fleix-disc single available with "Mummy", a fanzine.

Monks Of Doom
THE INSECT GOD
C/Z Records CZ 047
Includes **'Let's Split'**.

Neil The Hippy
NEIL'S HEAVY CONCEPT ALBUM
WEA WX12 (Vinyl only)
Novelty album by Nigel Planner, based on his character in TV comedy series *The Young Ones*. Includes **'The Gnome'**, which he also performed on TV.

The Not Quite
'Astronomy Domine'
Recorded as a demo, but unreleased.

Pink Floyd
UMMAGUMMA
EMI CDS 7 46404 8
Includes live versions of **'Astronomy Domine'** (and '**Set The Controls For The Heart Of The Sun**') with David Gilmour in Syd mode.
+
Unconfirmed reports claim that

Pink Floyd occasionally soundchecked with **'Arnold Layne'** on their 1987/8 tours!

REM
Orange Crush
WEA W2960CD (CD single)
+
Everybody Hurts
WEA W0169CD2 (CD single)
Both of the above feature the same version of **'Dark Globe'**, a studio recording which also appeared on a flexi-disc with *Sassy* magazine. REM have also performed the track live.

Rosebud/Discoballs
A TRIBUTE TO THE PINK FLOYD
Atlantic Records K50446 (LP)
French album of disco style cover versions, with **'Interstellar Overdrive'** and **'Arnold Layne'**.

Sanity Assassins
Blow Torch Love Doll
Tombstone Records T32 (American 7")
B-side is **'Take Up Thy Stethoscope and Walk'**, erroniously credited to "Barrett & Waters".

The Shamen.
STRANGE DAY DREAMS
Materiali Sonori MASO CD 90003
Italian CD including **'Golden Hair'** (formerly the B-side of their Young Till Yesterday 7" (Moksha SOMA1)); **'Long Gone'** (from the Wildwood tribute album) and a track credited, presumably by mistake, to S. Barrett, **'It's All Around'**.

Shockabilly
JUST BEAUTIFUL
Shimmy Disc SDE 8914CD
Live album, includes **'Lucifer Sam'**.

Sigmund Und Seine Freind
'See Emily Play'
Details unknown.

Smashing Pumpkins
'I Am One'
Hut Records HUTEN 18 (10" single)
B-side sis **'Terrapin'**, but only on this special edition.

The Soft Boys
Kingdom Of Love
Armageddon AEP 002 (7" single)
B-side is **'Vegetable Man'**, the unreleased Pink Floyd song.

Teenage Fan Club
THE KING
Creation Records CRE CD 096
Includes **'Interstellat Overdrive'**

This Mortal Coil
Blood
4AD DAD1005
Includes **'Late Night'**.

The Three O'Clock
BAROQUE HOEDOWN
Frontier 4605
Includes **'Astronomy Domine'**.

360's
Link Records
Details, including title, unknown.

Three To One
PEBBLES VOL. 14
Archive International Productions AIP 10014 (vinyl only)
'See Emily Play'
1960's Canadian cover version on 1980's various artists collection.

True West
'Lucifer Sam'
Details unknown.

Tyrnaround
SIX SONGS
Polyester Records
Australian release including **'Astronomy Domine'**.

The Urinals
'Arnold Layne'
Details unknown.

Voivod
NOTHINGFACE
Noise N0142 – 2
+
THE BEST OF VOIVOD,
Noise N0196 – 2
Both include **'Astronomy Domine'**.

The Walking Seeds
Gates Of Freedom
Paperhouse Records Paper #1 (7"
single)
B-side is an accented 'Astronomy
Dominé', with a label design
reflecting the rear sleeve of PIPER . . .

Weird Happenings Orchestra
'Interstellar Overdrive'
Performed live.

Various
**BEYOND THE WILDWOOD - A
TRIBUTE TO SYD BARRETT**
Imaginary Records ILLCD 001
No Good Trying (The Mock
Turtles); **Octopus** (Plasticland);
Arnold Layne (SS – 20); **Matilda
Mother** (Paul Roland); **She Took A
Long Cold Look** (Fit And Limo);
Long Gone (The Shamen); **If The
Sun Don't Shine** (Opal); **Baby
Lemonade** (The Ashes In The
Morning); **Wolfpack** (The Lobster
Quadrille); **Golden Hair** (The Paint
Set); **No Man's Land** (Tropicana
Fishtank); **Apples And Oranges**
(The T.V. Personalities); **Two Of A
Kind** (The Soup Dragons); **Scream
Thy Last Scream** (The Green
Telescope). Extra Tracks on CD:-See
Emily Play (The Chemistry Set);
Rats (What Noise); **Gigolo Aunt**
(Death of Samantha).
Included the unreleased (but
widely bootlegged) *'Scream Thy
Last Scream'* and a new song, *'If
The Sun Don't Shine'*, built around
the last section of Jugband Blues.

Overseas releases included picture
CDs and coloured vinyl. Each batch
of UK album sleeves was printed in
a different colour.
    Also recorded for the project, but
not used, were **Arnold Layne** (the
Avant Gardners); **Lucifer Sam** (Life
After Death); **Late Night** (Pure
Leuge) and **Jugband Blues (TV**
Personalities).

**FUCK YOUR DREAMS, THIS IS
HEAVEN**
Crammed Discs CRAM 048
Includes **Flaming** (Niki Mono and
Nikolas Klau); **No Mans Land**
(Peter Principle) and **Late Night**
(Minimal Compact).
    The album comprises the original
soundtrack to a film of the same
title, dedicated to Syd Barrett.

Film And Video
**TONITE LETS ALL MAKE LOVE
IN LONDON.**
Directed by Peter Whitehead.
Includes three segments of a
performance of **'Interstellar
Overdrive'**, one where Pink Floyd
are, briefly, seen playing. See For
Miles promise an 'eventual' release
on video.

THE COMMITTEE.
Directed by Peter Sykes.
Score by The Pink Floyd,
unreleased on record. Although
previewed for the press, and
occasionally hired out to film
societies, the film was never put on
general release.

**ROCK & ROLL - THE
GREATEST YEARS - 1967 (video)**
(Video Collection VC4085)
Includes a promo clip for 'See
Emily Play', with David Gilmour
deputising for Syd.

SAN FRANCISCO.
Directed by Anthony Stern.
24 Hours in the life of the
American City, compressed to fit
along side a 15 minute version of
'Interstellar Overdrive', recorded
before Pink Floyd signed to EMI.

MUSIC POWER.
Directed by Gerome Laperrousaz.
Unreleased documentary
including Frank Zappa jamming to
'Interstellar Overdrive' with post-
Barrett Pink Floyd at the Amougies
Festival, Belgium, on October 25,
1969.

PINK FLOYD - THE WALL.
Screenplay by Roger Waters,
directed By Alan Parker.
Despite the 'no persons living or
dead' cliché, several of "Pink's"
antics derrive from Syd's
breakdown.

SYD BARRETT'S FIRST TRIP
C Vex Films/Directed by Nigel
Lesmoir-Gordon.
Silent; running time: 12 minutes.
Nigel Lesmoir-Gordon's standard
8mm film of Syd on his first acid
trip in the Gog Magog Hills
outside Cambridge, now
transferred to video. Also includes
footge of Pink Floyd outside
Abbey Road Studios in 1967, just
after they'd signed with EMI.
Limited edition of 5,000.

Miscellany
Kevin Ayers
'Singing A Song In The Morning'
Although Syd did record guitar for
this song (when it went under the
title of **'Religious Experience'**), he
is not heard on the released
version.

The Beatles
'What's The News Mary Jane?'
Just to set the record straight, Syd
DOES NOT play on this
unreleased outtake, whatever the
bootleggers may claim, or however
they re-title it!

Marillion
SCRIPT FOR A JESTER'S TEAR
EMI CDP 7 46237 2
The sleeve of **'A Saucerful Of
Secrets'** lies on the floor of the
room depicted on the back cover.
Former singer Fish once proposed
a cover of **'Arnold Layne'** for his
SONGS FROM THE MIRROR
album, opting instead for Pink
Floyd's **'Fearless'**.

Piblokto!
**THINGS MAY COME AND
THINGS MAY GO, BUT THE
ART SCHOOL DANCE GOES
ON FOREVER**
Harvest SHVL 768 (Vinyl only)
Syd is one of several former Art
School students whose
photographs appear on the cover
of this album by Pete Brown's
band (see Bond & Brown, above).

Pink Floyd
**INTERVIEW PICTURE DISCS/
CDs**
Although several of these
unofficial releases use photographs
of Syd's Floyd, all feature much
later interviews with other Floyd
members.

**THE MICK ROCK PHOTO
SESSIONS**
UFO Records MROK – 1
May 1993
Limited edition (of 2,000) Box Set
containing: a lavish booklet of
photographs by Rock taken at the
same session as the shot which
appears on the cover of **THE
MADCAP LAUGHS** and never

previously published, plus text by Pete Anderson; a tee-shirt based on that worn by Syd for the session; a postcard of the album sleeve; a numbered certificate of authenticity; an (optional) copy of **MADCAP . . .** on CD (the Canadian release, for some reason). A companion volume on the BARRETT album is being compiled as this book goes to press.

Among the bands to take their names from Syd's work are The Effervescing Elephants and The Gigolo Aunts.

Books
(Foreign language publications and sheet music collections have been ommitted, unless of special interest)

BRICKS IN THE WALL
(Baton Press 1987)
Karl Dallas.

LE LIVRE DU PINK FLOYD
(Albin Michel 1978)
Alain Dister, Jacques Leblanc, Udo Woehrle
Although in French, this book is made up mainly of photographs, many of them otherwise unpublished.

THE MAKING OF THE MADCAP LAUGHS
(Privately published; re-printed by Opel fanzine)
Malcolm Jones
Self-explanetary booklet by the EMI Producer/ label boss.

PINK FLOYD
(Futura 1976)
Rick Saunders
Now deleted paperback containing no information which cannot be found in the more readily available publications listed here.

PINK FLOYD - A VISUAL DOCUMENTARY
(Omnibus 1980, 1983 and 1988)
Miles
A heavily illustrated Pink Floyd chronology, twice updated, which contains many interesting early shots of the Syd group.

SAUCERFUL OF SECRETS - THE PINK FLOYD ODYSSEY
(Harmony Books (USA)/ Sidgwick & Jackson (UK) 1991)
Nicholas Scaffner
The UK edition has fewer photographs and used an uncorrected manuscript. The US version is Schaffner's final draft.

WHERE IS THE MADCAP CALLED SYD?
Italian book with lyrics also in English. Came with free 7" or CD single, which would be regarded as a bootleg outside Italy.

Fan Magazines
TERRAPIN
The first Syd Barrett magazine. Folded in the 70's after internal squables, although the reason given was 'lack of Syd'.

OPEL
From the same stable as *The Amazing Pudding* and an able successor to *Terrapin*, lasting for 12 issues – all of which are now impossible to find.

THE AMAZING PUDDING
Although subtitled *The Pink Floyd and Roger Waters Magazine*, TAP took up the Barrett torch when Opel folded. Ran for 60 issues. Back issues -many with unique pictures of Syd – are still available from Andy Mabbett, 67, Cramlington Road, Great Barr, Birmingham B42 2EE, England. Send Self-Addressed Envelope

with stamp or International Reply
Coupon for details.

CLOWNS & JUGGLERS
UK magazine published in the
'80s.

FRIENDS OF SYD BARRETT
1990s American publication.

Any discography of this nature can
only be a snapshot of the full
picture. The authors/compiler
would be grateful for details of any
errors, ommisions or future
releases. Please write to them c/o
Omnibus Press or The Amazing
Pudding (see above).